BEYOND

Roses Are Red, Violets are Blue

A Practical Guide for Helping Students Write Free Verse

Benjamin Green

with

Anita Punla

Cottonwood Press, Inc.
Fort Collins, Colorado

Requests for permission should be addressed to:

Cottonwood Press, Inc.
107 Cameron Drive
Fort Collins, Colorado 80525
1-800-864-4297
www.cottonwoodpress.com

ISBN 1-877673-28-5

Printed in the United States of America

Table of Contents

Introduction 5
The Middleground Method 7
Before You Begin 13
- Capturing Student Interest by Reading Aloud 17
- Defining Poetry 18
- Metaphors and Similes 21
- Using Interesting Words 23
- Avoiding Clichés 25

Choosing a Subject and Word Gathering 27
- Object Poem 31
- Alphabet 35
- Numbers 39
- Food 43
- Geometry 47
- Halloween 51
- A Fruit or a Vegetable 55
- Favorite Activity 59
- Four Seasons 63
- Five W's and an H 67
- Pets 71
- Brothers and Sisters 75
- How-To 79
- Animals 83
- Music 87
- Work of Art 91
- Clothing Memory 95
- Sense of Place 99
- Parent's Hands 103
- Student Memory 107
- Anger 111
- A Verb and a Verb 115
- The Blazon 119
- Autobiographical Poem 123
- Model Poem 127
- Design a Poem 131

Extracting a Poem 135
Revising 139
Sharing 147
How to Prepare a Manuscript 151
Appendix 155

Other books by Benjamin Green

From a Greyhound Bus
The Lost Coast
The Field Notes of a Madman
Monologs from the Realm of Silence
This Coast of Many Colors
The Sound of Fish Dreaming

Other books by Anita Punla

Understudy, Learning from Nature's Strategies

Other books by Anita Punla and Benjamin Green

Green Grace, woman as earth landscape

INTRODUCTION

I am a poet. My work appears regularly in literary periodicals, and I have published six books of poetry.

I am also a school janitor. After receiving my B.A. in 1985, I decided not to pursue an advanced degree but to start, instead, a janitorial service. The work suits me; it leaves mornings available for my writing.

It has also led to my work in the classroom teaching poetry. Teachers at Pacific Union School in Arcata, California, learned that I am a poet and invited me to conduct poetry workshops in their classrooms. The first of these workshops consisted mostly of my reading, followed by a question and answer period. The results were satisfactory, but both teachers and students expected more. They wanted me to teach them *how* to write poetry.

I was hesitant. Being a janitor is a bit like being an archaeologist: every night I sift through the refuse and debris of a day's activities in the classroom, and what I have seen over the years has made me see how difficult it can be to teach poetry.

For example, I have seen a lot of what I call "blank page" exercises that give only broad, general instructions — "Write a poem" or "Write a poem about peace." Students seem to have a lot of problems getting started; they don't know what to write about or how to approach the topic.

I have seen a tendency toward plagiarism as well. When model poems are used, students mimic them too closely. Or sometimes they seem to write what they think the teachers want, rather than what they really feel.

Finally, I have seen a number of formulaic fill-in-the-blank exercises. (*Write a noun on the first line. On the second line, write two adjectives describing that noun. On the third line . . .*) A formula is not poetry, neither in process nor product. Students recognize this. Formulas only increase their uncertainty about what a poem is and how one is written.

What I wanted was a new approach to teaching students how to write poetry. Working in the classroom and testing my work with students, I developed what I call my "middleground method" — "middleground" because it lies somewhere in the middle of two extremes.

At one extreme is the "blank page" assignment, and at the other extreme is the "fill in the blank" exercise. The middleground method takes the best of the blank page exercise (freedom and spontaneity) and mixes it with the best of the formulaic exercise (structure and guided focus), while avoiding the worst of both methods (fear and boredom). It teaches poetry as a process, a process that probes the memory and taps the imagination. This book describes my approach and shows teachers how to use it.

The middleground method has been used successfully with students of all ages, from second grade through senior adults. Schools, libraries, senior centers and park and recreation programs have all offered middleground method workshops, with results that have been very rewarding to students, teachers and me. The poems written in these workshops are consistently of high quality. Students recognize their accomplishments and proudly share their poetry with peers, parents and others. Teachers value the method because it gives them a practical tool for teaching and helps them to know their students better.

The middleground method works. It is a process that teaches students to appreciate poetry, through the writing of quality poems. It gives teachers a way to bring poetry into the classroom, without frustration. It works because it uses structure to help free self-expression.

Program directors, teachers, students, workshop participants and individual writers are invited to submit poems written using the middleground method exercises in this book. All submissions will be considered for possible inclusion in future editions. I am especially interested in "Design a Poem" results (See page 131) for possible *new* exercises to include.

I also invite readers to write if they have any questions. Address all correspondence to:

Benjamin Green
c/o Cottonwood Press
107 Cameron Drive
Fort Collins, CO 80525

The Middleground Method

The Middleground Method In a Nutshell

1. Choosing a subject or idea and visualizing it.
2. Word gathering — collecting words, phrases, pieces of information, metaphors, images, descriptions, etc., to use later in the composition of the poem.
3. Extracting a poem — using material from word gathering to create a rough draft.
4. Revising the rough draft to create a finished poem.
5. Sharing — by reading aloud, publishing or exhibiting.

THE MIDDLEGROUND METHOD

The middleground method imitates how poets work. In a nutshell, it involves the following steps:

1. Choosing a subject or idea and visualizing it.
2. Word gathering — collecting words, phrases, pieces of information, metaphors, images, descriptions, etc., to use later in the construction of the poem.
3. Extracting a poem — using material from word gathering to create a rough draft.
4. Revising the rough draft to create a finished poem.
5. Sharing — by reading aloud, publishing or exhibiting.

The best way to learn about the middleground method is to try it, first on your own and then with your students. A good exercise to begin with is "Object Poem" (pages 31-34). It is quick, relatively easy, has a high rate of success and exposes the elements of the middleground method in an obvious way.

First read the teacher instructions and the student instructions for "Object Poem." Then complete the exercise for yourself, using the guidelines below to help you understand each step in the middleground method. As you complete a poem of your own, you will learn what to expect when you lead students through the process. You will experience firsthand what your students will experience, and you will be able to anticipate many of their questions.

Below is a brief explanation of each step in the middleground method for writing poetry.

Step One
Choosing a Subject

The first step in writing any poem is to decide upon a subject or idea. Poems are most effective when the subject has meaning for the poet. If the poet is bored with a topic, the poem will probably be boring as well. Encourage students to select topics they have strong feelings about (either positive or negative feelings) and that fit their own experience. The average sixth grader, for example, will write a better poem about "fighting with my big brother" than about "war." That's because war probably lies outside the student's experience.

Each of the poem-writing exercises in this book gives students a general subject. Then it asks them to narrow that subject to a specific topic that has meaning for them. Before they begin writing, students should spend time visualizing their subject, recalling memories and/or details about it and sometimes examining it from different angles and points of view.

Step Two
Word Gathering

Word gathering means collecting words, phrases, pieces of information, metaphors, images, descriptions, etc., to use later in the composition of a poem. Students may want to keep a special notebook or "wordbook" for word gathering, or they can simply use ordinary paper or a section of their notebook for the word gathering steps.

Each of the poem-writing exercises on pages 27-134 includes a number of word gathering steps for students to follow. The pages are designed so that you can make a transparency and go over the steps one at a time, using the overhead projector. (Other options, of course, include writing the steps on the blackboard, going over them orally or reproducing them as a hand-out.)

Each word gathering step includes a series of writing prompts for students to follow. Allow plenty of time for students to complete these prompts. (It's important to be flexible, but about five minutes per step works well.) Emphasize that there are no right or wrong answers to the prompts. Students may respond in paragraph form, in full sentences, in phrases or with lists of words. Ask them to respond as fully as possible, pushing themselves and stretching for more ideas.

The more words written in response to the prompts, the easier it will be to extract good lines later for the rough draft of a poem. You might use getting dressed in the morning as an analogy. If your closet contains only one pair of pants and a shirt, then you have little choice about what to wear. However, if the closet is full of clothes, it is a lot easier to make an excellent and appropriate selection for the day's activities.

Emphasize that responses to the prompts in each step should *not* take the form of a poem. At this point, students are not creating poems. They are warming up, developing ideas and collecting material.

For examples of word gathering responses from students for "Object Poem," see the Appendix, "The Middleground Method in Action," pages 157-161.

Step Three
Extracting a Poem

After students complete the responses to prompts, the extraction process begins. Extracting a poem consists of three parts:

Choosing the best words. The first step in the extraction process is to have students circle the "best" words from each step of their word gathering. Explain that the best words will be the ones that:

- give the most important and accurate information
- use the most interesting and original language
- create the most vivid pictures in the reader's mind
- "sound" the best

Using the best words to create the rough draft of a poem. After they have circled the best words and phrases, have students start creating lines for their poem, using the words they have circled. Ask them to create only one or two lines from each step, in the order the steps are given. (Assure students that they will be able to reword and rearrange their lines later, if they find it necessary.)

Because writing poetry is new to students, most will want to write full sentences that stretch from margin to margin. To keep them focused on writing verse, have them fold their writing paper in thirds. The narrow writing space helps them keep their lines short. You might also mention that lines of a poem are rarely more than eight or nine words long.

It is important to talk about the reasons for line breaks. Poets usually use a line break for these reasons:

- to let the reader take a breath
- to indicate that the reader should pause
- to slow down the poem with short lines or speed it up with long lines
- to form a certain pattern on the page or to stress certain words by putting them at the beginning or at the end of a line.

Encourage students to keep their poems short, tight and concentrated. Dynamism and tension are created when poems are kept short. By choosing only one or two lines to include, per prompt, students learn to discriminate between their best writing and their weaker writing. (You might return to the clothes closet analogy: even with a full closet, a person still has to choose the best outfit; he or she can't wear three pairs of pants and six shirts at one time.)

Playing with the rough draft and creating a not-so-rough draft. Before students are finished with the extraction step, they need to play with their lines until the poem reads smoothly and makes sense. In other words, they need to take their rough draft and turn it into a not-so-rough draft. Students, before they complete the extracting step, should have a not-so-rough draft they are willing to share and take to the next step, revising.

For examples of student work in completing the extraction step, see the Appendix, "The Middleground Method in Action," pages 157-161.

Step Four
Revising

The next step in the middleground method is revising — a necessary and important part of the writing process. Revising means literally "to see again" and to see through the reader's eyes. Too often students think what they have written is good, not because it *is* good but because they have written it. Students must realize that their not-so-rough drafts are only a beginning that can be made better.

While word gathering allows students to be spontaneous and personal, revising is more impersonal. It switches the focus from the writer's experience to the words that describe that experience.

The first part of the revision process is to have students use questions from the "Revision Checklist" (page 143) to take a second look at their poems. Using the questions from the checklist to guide them, students should first revise their work on their own.

Next they can get feedback from others. Before the high school level, that feedback will likely be from you, the teacher. (Response groups are not usually useful with younger students because they are not yet at a developmental level where they are able to judge the quality of another's work, or even their own work. If they are used, response groups should be as a supplement to teacher feedback.)

Revision is the chance to change one's mind. After completing the "Revision Checklist" and listening to the feedback of others, a student may want to make adjustments. He or she may want to add new ideas and/or new details, or to delete words and images that do not contribute to the poem's momentum.

A student may even discover that what is written does not, after all, express his or her ideas and feelings. If so, the student may choose to try the steps in "A Second Way to Look at Revision" (page 145). The techniques in this list provide very effective ways to approach the poem in a totally different way.

The revision process should continue until the work is finished. You should allow plenty of time for the process because real revision may take weeks, months or even years. (See also "Revising," page 139.)

Step Five
Sharing

No writing is complete until it is shared. Sharing can take many forms, including classroom and public readings and publishing in newspapers, magazines, books, classroom anthologies or personal collections. Students can also share by exhibiting their work in school and public displays or by creating posters and other forms of artwork that incorporate poetry. (See also "Sharing," page 147.)

Before you begin using the middleground method with your students, you may want to review with them the material in the next chapter, "Before You Begin."

Before You Begin

BEFORE YOU BEGIN

The following sections set the stage for teaching poetry with the middleground method. Depending upon the age, experience and skill level of your students, you may want to try any or all of the following before you begin:

Capturing Student Interest by Reading Aloud 17
Defining Poetry 18
Metaphors and Similes — Student Instructions 21
Using Interesting Words — Student Instructions 23
Avoiding Clichés — Student Instructions 25

Capturing Student Interest by Reading Aloud

An excellent way to introduce poetry in the classroom is by reading poems aloud. The poem itself is the best teaching tool available.

Students enjoy writing poems more if they first enjoy reading and hearing them. Reading aloud (or listening to audio tapes) makes poetry immediately pleasurable. When students read a poem silently to themselves, often stumbling in their efforts, they hear nothing. When they hear the poem read aloud, they experience the poem at its best. They hear the pacing, the pauses. They enjoy the words. Moreover, reading poetry creates a receptive mood in the classroom and serves as a reminder that poetry is an oral tradition.

When you read poems to your students, choose poems they will enjoy. Select poems that relate to young people's experiences, with vocabulary appropriate to their developmental level. I find the most success with poems that describe natural phenomena or personal experiences, poems they can understand on the first hearing. Two widely available sources mentioned often in this book are *The Norton Anthology of Modern Poetry* (W.W. Norton & Company, Inc., 1988) and, for works more suitable for younger students, *Piping Down the Valleys Wild* (Bantam Doubleday Dell Books for Young Readers: New Yearling Edition, 1982).

Poems are seen as well as heard. Provide students with copies of the poems you read, using transparencies on the overhead or writing poems on the blackboard. As they listen, have students write down words that stand out. These will be the words that are fresh, powerful and interesting.

Most of the exercises in this book include suggested readings. Depending upon the skill level and maturity of your students, reading aloud and discussing some of these poems can be an excellent introduction to each exercise.

Defining Poetry

Over the years, many people have defined poetry in many different ways. "What Is Poetry?" (page 20) gives a number of different definitions and provides food for thought and discussion.

The middleground method uses a simple and effective definition of poetry from an obvious source — the dictionary. *Webster's New Collegiate* calls a poem "**a composition in verse that communicates the sense of a complete experience**." This definition is the starting point for the middleground method.

Let's look at the various pieces of this definition:

A composition. First, a poem is a composition, or an arrangement of words that a writer has chosen carefully in order to achieve a certain effect. It shows and describes, using images and mental pictures. In a way, you might think of a composition as a painting in words.

Verse. A poem is written in verse — short, rhythmic phrases that may or may not rhyme. Verse is, in fact, another name for poetry. In a poem, lines are arranged to emphasize the musical quality of language.

It is important to note that poems and song lyrics are not the same thing, although both are written in verse. A lyric is meant to be sung; the words work along with the melody. A poem stands alone.

One way to help students see the difference is to play a tape of a poet reading in another language. (Example: Czeslaw Milosz, the Polish Nobel Prize winner, reading a poem in Polish.) When they hear a poem in a foreign language, the meaning of words does not get in the way of the students' listening. Instead of words, they hear the *sounds* of the words — the rhymes, the repetition, the alliteration, the timing and the rhythmic beat, all in the cadence of natural speech. They begin to see how poems emphasize the musical quality of language with the words themselves.

Any discussion of verse also brings up the issue of free verse. Free verse does not follow conventional metrical or stanzaic patterns. It has either irregular rhyme or no rhyme at all and, instead of the regular metrical rhythms of traditional poetry, has more natural rhythms based on the cadences of speech. Free verse originated with certain poets who wanted to create their own rules about verse, based upon patterns of thought, breath rhythms and visual appearance.

To understand how free verse relates to the other forms of poetry, you might give a ten minute history. Start by reading a chant. The Navajo "Beauty" chant is a good example. This can be found in a number of books, including *Pieces of White Shell — A Journey to Navajo Land,* by Terry Tempest Williams (University of New Mexico Press, 1987). Chants exemplify the original nature of poetry: strong beat and repetition.

To demonstrate strict meter and rhyme, read a sonnet by William Shakespeare. Go on to Walt Whitman, whose poetry breaks away from rhyme and strict meter while maintaining a strong momentum of rhythm. Finally, William Carlos Williams' short free verse poems introduce students to the modern era of poetry writing.

Communication. A poem is an act of communication. With a poem, the poet conveys a message — either to oneself, to particular others or to a generalized audience. The poet takes an idea and turns it into an image, into something that can be grasped by the senses as well as the intellect. (See also Metaphors and Similes, page 21.) For example, instead of saying, "I feel lonely," the writer *shows* loneliness with images that evoke loneliness, like "overgrown fence posts" or "mailboxes closed with spider webs."

Poetry communicates with words and the images they create. It also communicates with the silence between words, the pause between thoughts, the white space that surrounds and intrudes on the images. Much of what a poem communicates is in what is *not* said within the poem.

Experience. Poetry communicates the sense of a complete experience. It allows writers to stand back from their experience, to recall it, to relate to it deeply, to express it and to assign it a value it might not otherwise have.

Communicating the experience involves both subjective and objective elements. In describing a sunrise, for example, a writer might include facts that can be observed objectively, like time, temperature, weather, location and visible colors. An objective description might read, "5:30 in the morning; 45 degrees; wet, gray fog obscures the sun."

The subjective experience of dawn might include emotions, moods and opinions.: "I was grouchy to be wakened so soon, only to stand in a sodden mist."

A poem is a composition in verse
that communicates the sense of a complete experience.

What Is Poetry?

Poetry is "a way of saying what you don't know." — Marvin Bell

Poetry is "a series of explanations of life." — Carl Sandburg

Poetry is human speech made musical. — Anonymous

A poem is language worth preserving. — Anonymous

Poetry is the spontaneous overflow of powerful feelings. — William Wordsworth

Poetry is the art of uniting pleasure with beauty by calling imagination to the help of reason. — Samuel Johnson

Poetry is indefinable, and unmistakable. — Edwin A. Robinson

Poetry is the record of the best and happiest moments of the happiest and best minds. — Percy Shelley

Poetry is the suggestion, by the imagination, of noble grounds for the noble emotions. — John Ruskin

Poetry is not a thing said but a way of saying it. — A.E. Housman

Poetry, like life, states that the very self of a thing is its relations. — Eli Siegel

A complete poem is one where an emotion has found its thought and the thought has found the words. — Robert Frost

A poem is the condensed symbolic articulation of life. — Anonymous

Metaphors and Similes

Don't let the words "metaphor" and "simile" scare you. They are just fancy words for something we do all the time: compare two essentially unlike things. For example, if we say, "That dog is as ugly as mud," we are comparing a dog to mud. If we say, "That mulberry tree is an old friend," we are comparing the tree to a friend.

For a quick lesson in simile and metaphor, just try putting a frightened child to bed. Tree branches become the arms of hideous monsters. Bed posts become old bones. Clothes on the floor are dead bodies. The closet is a cave full of unsavory creatures, and dust bunnies under the bed are transformed into trolls.

Poets and other writers use simile and metaphor to make strong impressions on their readers. For example, a writer could say, "Tory's dad is quite grumpy in the morning." But if she really wanted to drive home her point, she might say, "Tory's dad is a grizzly before his first cup of coffee." While the first sentence gives the correct information, the second does more. It creates a picture or image.

What is the difference between a simile and metaphor? A simile is a comparison that uses the words "like" or "as." Some examples:

- *The kitten purred like a locomotive.*
- *Sometimes my sister is like a gnat buzzing around my face.*
- *My algebra teacher is as cranky as a cat who suddenly sees a Doberman pinscher strolling up the walk.*

A metaphor, on the other hand, does *not* use the words "like" or "as." Instead, it states that one thing *is* another thing. (In general, metaphors are stronger, more forceful, than similes.) Some examples:

- *Mario's smile is a magnet.*
- *Jana's old Yankees' hat was a tarnished halo.*
- *Winter evenings in front of the fireplace are heaven.*
- *I was lying in the hammock, my cradle.*

Don't worry too much about whether an expression is a simile or a metaphor when you are writing. The important thing is to *use* similes and metaphors. Let your imagination run wild. You don't have to be completely literal and state the actual truth; instead, you can play with language. You can be creative. A straightforward statement like this is fine:

My dad is a good cook.

However, this metaphor is a lot more interesting:

My dad is Betty Crocker in Birkenstocks.

Try your hand at writing similes and/or metaphors by completing the sentences below. Be creative and free as you come up with truly original comparisons.

1. Getting up for school in the morning is like . . .
2. Family vacations are . . .
3. The nurse's earrings dangled like . . .
4. Taking a math test is like . . .
5. My best friend is . . .

Write a simile or metaphor about each subject below. Keep in mind the mood or opinions you want to convey. For example, if you want to show that you really *like* your bedroom, don't compare it to a rat-infested prison.

1. Your bedroom.
2. One of your relatives.
3. A favorite activity.
4. A task or chore you dislike doing.
5. Winter.

Now write three more similes or metaphors about three subjects of your choice.

Using Interesting Words

Poems are filled with interesting words — specific, clear words that create pictures in your readers' minds.

Suppose you want to describe a friend walking down the street. If you say, "My friend was walking down the street," you aren't creating much of a picture. What street is it? Elm Street, Buttonwood Drive, the Interstate? What is your friend wearing? A plaid sport coat, an oversized trench coat from Goodwill, a Penn State sweatshirt with axle grease on the sleeve? Is he chewing gum, or is he "snapping his strawberry Bubbalicious to the beat of Bob Marley"?

Try your hand at creating word pictures. Replace the bland words below with more interesting details.

1. house
2. dog
3. blue jeans
4. flower
5. music

It is especially important to use interesting verbs when you write. The best way to punch up your verbs is simply by replacing them with more accurate or specific ones. Instead of saying, "Luisa *ran* down the stairs," you could say "Luisa *darted* down the stairs."

Although the best way to make a verb more specific is by replacing it with a more interesting verb, sometimes you just can't find the right one. That's when you call in the adverbs. Adverbs are words that describe verbs. (Examples: She walked *softly* into the kitchen. He took the key *slyly.*) Improve the sentences below either by replacing the verbs with new ones or by using adverbs.

1. Ellen *drank* her coffee.
2. Dale *went* to New Orleans.

3. Janice *wrote* the phone number on the note pad.
4. The hungry baby *cried.*
5. My mom *told* us to *walk* to the store.
6. Three-year-old Luke *drew* a picture on the wall.
7. Paula *lifted* the barbell.
8. Jeff *crossed* the street.

Now use all your knowledge of precise and interesting words to rewrite the paragraph below.

Leanne woke up to her alarm clock one morning. She was still tired. She went downstairs and got some food. Then her mom came down in her robe. She was tired, too. Leanne finished her breakfast just as her brother came into the room. He was loud and unhappy. He irritated everyone. Leanne was happy to leave for school. She got her lunch and left.

Finally, write a short description of something that happened to Leanne on her way to school. Use what you have learned about interesting language.

Avoiding Clichés

Clichés are those worn-out phrases that everybody uses all the time. A few examples:

- *as red as a rose*
- *as strong as an oak tree*
- *sparkled like diamonds*
- *light as a feather*

Sometimes clichés can become a habit. It's easier to say, "She ran like the wind" than it is to think of something original, like "She ran as fast as a taxi on a New York freeway." Using a cliché is easier than coming up with something new and fresh, but it's boring.

Avoiding clichés requires a certain independence. Let go of everything you have been taught about the world. Think of yourself as a child, seeing the world for the first time with wide open eyes and a wide open mind.

Rewrite the clichés below. Be funny or serious, witty or wise, but be original.

1. His hands were cold as ice.
2. We were packed into the car like sardines.
3. She is as strong as an ox.
4. His tummy shook like a bowlful of Jell-O.
5. It was a dark and stormy night.

Now read the paragraph below. Identify all the clichés.

I felt lazy as a sloth that afternoon. It was hot as a desert outside, and by the time I pulled myself off the couch and over to the window, it was also raining cats and dogs. There was no way I was going to walk the dog in the rain. He would just have to wait.

Besides, I needed something to eat. I hadn't eaten for a full hour, and I was so hungry I could eat a horse. (Mom says if I keep eating so often, I'll be as big as a house, but what does she know?) I looked around in the refrigerator for five or ten minutes before I realized that finding a candy bar in the midst of all those rotting vegetables would be like looking for a needle in a haystack. As luck would have it, Dad walked in before I'd shut the refrigerator door. True to character, he said it, his all-time favorite phrase: "Are you getting something to eat or trying to cool down the whole house? Electricity costs money, you know. Do you think money grows on trees?"

Rewrite the paragraph, replacing the clichés you underlined with more creative language.

Choosing a Subject and Word Gathering

26 Exercises that Help Students Create Poems

Choosing a Subject and Word Gathering

The 26 exercises that follow lead students through the first two stages of the middleground method: choosing a subject and word gathering. For examples of actual student work in completing these steps, see the Appendix, "The Middleground Method in Action," pages 157-161.

Choosing a Subject
A Review

Poems are most effective when the subject has meaning for the poet. If the poet is bored with a topic, the poem will probably be boring as well. Encourage students to select topics that they have strong feelings about — either positive or negative feelings. Encourage them to select topics that fit their own experience. The average sixth grader, for example, will write a better poem about "fighting with my big brother" than about "war." That's because war probably lies outside the student's experience.

Each of the exercises that follow gives students a general subject. Then it asks them to narrow that subject to a specific topic that has meaning for them. Before they begin writing, students should spend some time visualizing their subject, recalling memories and/or details about it and sometimes examining it from different angles and points of view.

Word Gathering
A Review

Word gathering involves collecting words, phrases, pieces of information, metaphors, images, descriptions, etc., to use later in the construction of a poem. Students may want to keep a special notebook or "wordbook" for word gathering, or they can simply use ordinary paper or a section of their notebook for the word gathering steps.

Each of the exercises that follow includes a number of word gathering steps for students to follow. These pages are designed so that you can make a transparency and go over the steps, one at a time, using the overhead projector. (Other options, of course, include writing the steps on the blackboard, going over them orally or reproducing them as a handout.)

Each word gathering step includes a series of writing prompts. Allow plenty of time for students to complete these prompts. (It's important to be flexible, but about five minutes per step works well.) Emphasize that there are no right or wrong answers to the prompts. Students may respond in paragraph form, in full sentences, in phrases or with lists of words. Ask them to respond as fully as possible, pushing themselves and stretching for more ideas.

The more words written in response to the prompts, the easier it will be to extract good lines later for the rough draft of a poem. You might use getting dressed in the morning as an analogy. If your closet contains only one pair of pants and a shirt, then you have little choice about what to wear. However, if the closet is full, it's a lot easier to make an excellent and appropriate selection for the day's activities.

Emphasize that responses to the prompts in each step should *not* take the form of a poem. At this point, students are not creating poems. They are warming up, developing ideas and collecting material.

Object Poem

With "Object Poem," students write a poem describing an object, any object that holds some meaning for them. Ask students to choose their objects in advance and to bring them to school for this exercise. (You may also want to have an assortment of interesting objects available for students who forget, or who can't bring their objects to class.)

Notes

The object poem can be repeated at the end of the school year to see how much progress students have made in the writing of poems.

Suggested readings

Piping Down the Valleys Wild

"The Balloon," Karla Kuskin, page 6

"The Lonely Scarecrow," James Kirkup, page 69

Object Poem

Choose an object that you value in some way for the subject of your poem. It might be an object you cherish, or it might be an object that you just find appealing in some way.

Look at this object — really look at it. Use all your senses to focus on details. Look at the object from different perspectives, perhaps from a distance or with a magnifying glass. Speak to it. Listen to it "talk back." Observe the object at different times and under different conditions.

Then begin the word gathering steps below. Word gathering involves gathering words and ideas to use later in writing your poem. Don't worry now about what your final poem will be like. Let the words flow, and write as much as possible for each step in the time allowed.

Word gathering

Step 1: Where did you find the object? Where did it come from? Describe place and setting.

Example: *The old kitchen timer came from our kitchen junk drawer. The dark, cluttered junk drawer is stuffed with birthday candles, shish-kebab spears, twist ties, broken refrigerator magnets and millions of other odds and ends.*

Step 2 Describe the object. What is its size, shape, color, weight, texture, taste, odor, etc.?

Example: *The timer is about the size of a baseball and the weight of an egg. Its smooth white plastic is melted on one side, where a hot pan touched it. It ticks loudly.*

Step 3 Alter your perspective and describe the object further. For example, you might turn the object inside out, wear a blindfold as you examine it, look at it from a distance, hold it close to your face or stand over it and look at it from above.

Example: *With its upturned face, it looks like a gruff little drill sergeant standing at attention and barking out seconds to my mother.*
From a distance, it looks like an ice cream cone starting to melt.

Step 4: Describe how the object is like you. What do you have in common? Think about personality traits, physical characteristics, experiences, etc.

Example: *not perfect, like me*
We're both short and demanding.
Both of us spend a lot of time in the kitchen and neither of us wants to.

Step 5: Describe how the object is like your mother or father. What do they have in common? Think about personality traits, physical characteristics, experiences, etc.

Example: *The timer's face is shiny, like my dad's nose after a game of baseball.*
It's always paying attention to time, like my mom.

Step 6: What does this object mean to you? What does it represent or symbolize? Out of all the objects you could have chosen, why did you choose to write about this particular one?

Example: *I like its interesting, melted look.*
It makes me mad because it's always taking away my mom's attention.

Step 7: Name the object. Simply state what it is.

Example: *A kitchen timer.*

Now you are ready to go on to the next stages of writing your poem. See "Extracting a Poem," "Revising" and "Sharing" (pages 135-153).

GRANDMA'S STATUE

Grandma's front room
amidst the gold-gilded mirror and
Impressionist painting,
fake grapes and tasseled lamp shades.
    Proudly she stood,
on top of the sea foam green carpet.

Half my size and twice my weight.
Roman goddess frozen in time
pouring water from a big curved pot.

Perhaps an ancient marble sculpture
    chiseled by an Italian artist
    and later stolen from Roman ruins.
More likely a cheap replica
    molded from plaster in a factory
    and later bought at a flea market.

At night,
I lay on the brocade green couch.
She grows and becomes real.
No longer hard and white,
now soft and tan,
with golden curls and deep sea blue eyes,
a breezy white gown
    cinched with a gold cord,
turquoise water flows
    from the terra-cotta pot.

So golden and glamourous
    Me — so brown and plain.
A grown woman
    Me — a small girl.

More like my Grandma —
    a real life Venus.
    Strong. Beautiful. Poised.
Statue of a Roman goddess.

— Marie DiPrince, college student

CROSS

Around my neck,
Metal bonds —
A gift from my parents.

Glittering metal, tiny circles of gold,
dangling dagger —
Lightweight but its ideas are as
heavy as rocks.

A sign of purity and freedom,
a golden sword and chain,
safe from the superficial evil
of a
fearful society.

We reflect meaning and hope.
Strong,
often taken for granted.

Like my parents, symbol of love,
a treasure,
a gift to cherish.

Shiny disposition
seems to
shield out harm.

A golden cross and chain.

— Carlos Giron, high school student

Alphabet

With "Alphabet," students focus on a specific letter of the alphabet, looking at its appearance and comparing the letter to images in the world around them.

In order to cover the whole alphabet, you may want to assign a specific letter to each student.

Project Ideas

It is easy to have the class create an "abecedary" (alphabet book) by having students create graphic representations of their letters, to accompany their poems. It is helpful to have magazines, newspapers, children's books and art catalogs available, to give students ideas. You might also remind them of all the visual images of letters on the alphabet segments of "Sesame Street."

When all the poems and illustrations are complete, post them in alphabetical order around the room, or create an abecedary that students might take home to younger brothers and sisters or give to a kindergarten class.

ALPHABET

Remember watching "Sesame Street" and all those features about different letters of the alphabet: the little red typewriter on wheels, the letters that walk across the screen and the guy who paints letters of the alphabet on park benches, the bottoms of shoes and bald heads?

Now it's your turn to feature a letter of the alphabet, by writing a poem.

Take the letter you are going to use for your poem, and write it down on a piece of paper. Make it uppercase, lowercase or cursive — your choice.

Now look at the letter, really *look* at it. Look at it from every angle.

Then begin the word gathering steps below. Remember that word gathering involves gathering words and ideas to use later in writing your poem. Don't worry now about what your final poem will be like. Let the words flow, and write as much as possible for each step.

WORD GATHERING

Step 1: What does your letter look like? Describe its appearance. Then create a simile or metaphor that compares the letter to an image in nature.

Example: *C is the last quarter of the moon.*

Step 2: Create a second simile or metaphor by telling how the image you created sounds, smells, feels or tastes.

Example: *C sounds like the moon sighing.*

Step 3: List colors that start with your letter. (You may want to refer to the dictionary or an art supply catalog.) Choose colors that fit the images you created in Steps 1 and 2.

Example: *Charcoal — the color of the night sky*

Step 4: List words that start with your letter. Choose words that have a meaningful relationship to the images you created in Steps 1, 2 and 3.

Example: *clouds, comets, cold, cumulus, cool*

Step 5: Choose the four words you like best from Step 4. Use one of the words to create a new sentence about the image you have created.

Example: *Clouds drifted in front of the sighing moon.*

Step 6: Using one or more of the same four words, create a final sentence for your poem.

Example: *It was cool and then cold when the moon went into hiding.*

Now you are ready to go on to the next stages of writing your poem. See "Extracting a Poem," "Revising" and "Sharing" (pages 135-153).

S

the letter s is curving, curly
smooth, slivering
shining, slinking

sounds like a shooting star
feels like satin
smells like cinnamon
tastes like sugar

s is a shining star
a snowstorm
a silver screen

s is a smile
s is a scream
s is silly
s is sad

s is a street scattered with shadows
s is a skipping kid sister
s is a sunbeam shining on a salty sea

— Annie Mackey, 8th grade

F

The F on my report card
looks like a tommy gun
with a clip.
F stands for flunked, failed,
got fired and fell in a hole
during school.
— Dave Edwards, 6th grade

M

Two mountains with a valley,
A snake slithering.
M vibrates off your lips.
Mmmmmm.
Chocolate chip cookies.
M and M candies.
Flowing chocolate.
A sunset of mauve, maroon and magenta.
Magic, mysterious, miraculous, merry,
Meticulous, magnificent . . .
— Miranda Cook, 8th grade

F
is a rake
with which you continually rake up dead fronds.
That dead old tree cracks,
starts to fall
in flames,
the fronds are making a weird
flaming red and orange.
The tree is going to hit you.
All is quiet.
The flames are gone.
So are you.
— Sean Donohoe, 6th grade

NUMBERS

With "Numbers," students create a poem by looking at the visual properties of a number. They look only at the number's *appearance*, not its meaning.

PROJECT IDEAS

Students may enjoy creating "pictures" of their numbers, to display along with their poems. You might consider having their creations displayed in a math classroom or even at a local business.

NUMBERS

Even if you hate math, you can enjoy writing a poem about a number. All you have to do is think of the number as a shape, not as something to add up or divide or multiply.

Choose a positive integer for your poem — in other words, any whole number. (Single digit numbers are easier to work with.)

Write your number on a piece of paper, and study its appearance closely. Then begin the word gathering steps below. Remember to choose words that create images or pictures in your mind. Remember also that word gathering is just your first step in the process of writing a poem.

WORD GATHERING

Step 1: Spell out the name of your number. This name will become the title of your poem.

Example: *Eight*

Step 2: Describe the number, looking at only its appearance, not its meaning. What does it look like? Look at both the white space around the number and the dark space of the number itself. What shapes do you see?

Examples: *circles sitting on top of each other*
pools of white surrounded by rings of black

Step 3: Create a metaphor by comparing the number to something in your world.

Examples: *The number 8 is the toy race track my little brother got for Christmas.*
Eight is two rocks in the stream at the edge of town.

Step 4: Manipulate the number to change how it looks, doing whatever you like to alter its appearance. You might shade in an empty space or turn the number upside down, for example. Describe how you changed the number.

Example: *I turned my 8 on its side and squashed it.*

Step 5: Describe the new shape you have created. What does it resemble now? Create a second metaphor describing the new look.

Examples: *My squashed 8 is now two puddles of water.*
My squashed 8 is the tiny skid marks left by toy hot rods.

Now you are ready to go on to the next stages of writing your poem. See "Extracting a Poem," "Revising" and "Sharing" (pages 135-153).

ONE

A tall, lanky figure,
A towering street light,
The thin black line stands tall,
Surrounded by white nothingness.
With a single blow
I knock it to the ground.
A stick of licorice
Waiting to be devoured.

— Zac Curtis, high school

ZERO

Like a lone hole
in a sea of holes
waiting for someone
to step in it.
Twist it to make an 8,
an eightball.
The first number,
the leader,
the captain,
the chief:
ready for war
or ready for peace.

— Nick Newman, 5th grade

NINE

A small ball
climbing
a horizontal line
wide open space awaits
just inside the barriers
of the black circle.
Nine
is the old worn down baseball and bat
that my friends and I
played with after school.
I turn my nine on its side
so the circle is on the underside
of the one horizontal line
that is now vertical
I then roll the ball to the middle
so the line is
perfectly balanced
My nine is now
the old wooden seesaw
I once played on
for hours at a time
with my older brothers.

— Zachary Howard, 9th grade

With "Food," students write a poem about a favorite food. They concentrate on using their five senses to describe the food and the pleasure of eating it.

Suggested Readings

Piping Down the Valleys Wild

"Miss T.," Walter de la Mare, page 25

"Mummy Slept Late and Daddy Fixed Breakfast," John Ciardi, page 26

"Some Cook!" John Ciardi, page 28

"Catherine," Karla Kuskin, page 97

Food

Imagine that one of your favorite foods is sitting right in front of you on your desk. Imagine eating that food.

Think about how the food plays with all your senses. What does it *look* like? When you pick it up to take a bite, how does the food *feel*? Do you *hear* anything as you take a bite, like a crunch? How does the food *smell*? How does it *taste*?

Keep the images in your mind as you begin a poem about your favorite food. Start with the word gathering steps below. Remember that word gathering involves collecting words, phrases and sentences about your subject. The point is to write as much as possible and not to worry about doing it "right." You should concentrate on getting interesting details down on paper. Later you will choose the best words and phrases for your final poem.

Word Gathering

Step 1: Imagine that you live in the land of your favorite food. Write a statement about that food, being sure to include the name of the food in your sentence.

Example: *I could exist forever on just linguini.*

Step 2: Describe your food. What are its parts, traits, characteristics, ingredients, etc.? Try to include as many senses as possible in your description.

Example: *Long, lean linguini smells like it slithered through a nest of garlic.*

Step 3: Describe how to eat your favorite food. Be specific. Try to use strong, interesting verbs.

Example: *I twirl the linguini around on my fork and then slurp.*

Step 4: If your food could think, what would its thoughts be?

Example: *The strands of linguini nervously wait for the moment when I will plop a giant meatball on top of them. They are worried about being squashed.*

Step 5: How does your food make you hunger for it? What does it "do"? Remember, you don't have to think logically here. Use your imagination.

Example: *Basil and garlic leap out of the sauce and yank me to the table.*

Step 6: Is there something people should know about your food? If so, tell what.

Example: *Linguini is dangerous. It's as addictive as nicotine.*

Now you are ready to go on to the next stages of writing your poem. See "Extracting a Poem," "Revising" and "Sharing" (pages 135-153).

I live in the land of ice cream cones;
vanilla, chocolate, rocky road, pecan
praline, cookie dough, peanut butter
cup . . .
sugar cones, waffle cones, plain.

First, you lick the top of the ice cream
with your tongue, keep it smooth,
don't let it drip.
When you reach the cone, use your
teeth, start to bite, freeze to roof
of your mouth. Continue until near the
bottom of the cone; then, suck it dry.
Throw the tip of the cone into the trash
or feed it to birds on the street.

Cold thoughts, but sweet,
offer promises of total satisfaction.
Usually lies.

People with beards should know this:
when allowed to dry in the mustache,
ice cream becomes hard and sticky,
it smells and tastes very bad.

I know. My dad has a beard
and he eats a lot of ice cream.
He kisses me every night
when I go to sleep.
Yuck!

— Natalie Jones, 5th grade

I live in the land
of chocolate chip cookies;
in a place full of flour
and semi-sweet chocolate chips;
in a world of margarine and sugar,
eggs and vanilla, baking soda and whey.
I live in the land of fat greed,
where handfuls of crunchy cookies
are stuffed into chewing,
cavity-filled mouths,
where crumbs dribble down chins
onto shirt fronts and onto floors.
Chocolate chip cookies seem happy, but
they are short-lived.
Their skin is tan and oozes melted
chocolate.
The taste begins with the smell,
the tongue waters,
but you should know this:
no one really knows what
a chocolate chip cookie tastes like
for they are eaten too quickly.

— Kassi Kalen, 5th grade

With "Geometry," students look at geometric shapes and features in the natural landscape to create a poem.

Before you begin, ask students to make a list of geometric shapes. They will probably be able to think of a large number of them. If not, you might suggest additions from the list below, or have students take a look at the glossary of their math textbooks.

circle	pentagon	cylinder
triangle	hexagon	cone
square	octagon	sphere
rectangle	cube	rhombus
trapezoid	pyramid	diamond

It's a good idea to have a large number of nature photographs available for students. These can be actual photographs, posters or nature books. Students can look at the photographs for ideas when they are writing their similes and metaphors.

Another suggestion is to provide string. If some students have trouble manipulating their shapes in Step 3 (Student Instructions), they can create their shapes from string and then physically manipulate them by moving the string.

You don't have to know a thing about geometry to write a poem about a geometric shape. You just need to allow yourself to look at things differently. Remove the *meaning* from what you are seeing and look at shapes.

For example, take a look at one of your books. Don't think about what's inside the book, or about the homework you have on page 72. Instead, focus only on the shape you see. You will probably find that the cover of the book is a rectangle.

Choose a geometric shape as the subject of your poem. Then complete the word gathering steps below. Try to collect as many words, sentences and phrases as possible, even though you won't use all of them in your final poem. Don't worry right now about finding the perfect words. Open your mind to seeing shapes and letting the words flow.

WORD GATHERING

Step 1: Describe the geometric shape you have chosen. Don't use mathematical language. Just describe what you see.

Example: *A triangle is two lines sloping to a sharp point.*

Step 2: Create a simile or metaphor by comparing the shape to something in nature.

Example: *The triangle looks like the peaks in the Trinity Alps.*

Step 3: In your mind or on paper, manipulate the shape to change how it looks, doing whatever you like to change its appearance. Then describe how you changed the shape.

Examples: *I squashed my circle to make an oval.*
I lifted one side of my triangle to make an open box.

Step 4: If the new figure is a true geometric shape, tell what it is. If it is not a geometric shape, describe it in non-mathematical language.

Examples: *I now have a square.*
I now have a round ball with a pinched edge on one side.

Step 5: Describe the appearance of the manipulated shape. What does it resemble in nature? Create a simile or metaphor that describes the resemblance.

Examples: *A rhombus is the reflection of the Trinity Alps in a calm lake.*
A triangle with a lifted side is like the opening to a dark cave.

(Optional)
Step 6: Compare and contrast the metaphors you created in Steps 2 and 5. How could the two be related?

Example: *The Trinity Alps hide many dark caves.*

Now you are ready to go on to the next stages of writing your poem. See "Extracting a Poem," "Revising" and "Sharing" (pages 135-153).

TRIANGLE

Triangle:
a closed three sided shape;
a mountain, tall and pointed,
steep and still.
Put it on its side,
it becomes a baseball pennant
flying in the air
at a stadium.
A fan sits at a
Colorado Rockies' baseball game.

— Nick Newman, 5th grade

CIRCLE

Circle
a set of points equidistant from a center
a hole in a tree
the earth spinning around
the light reflecting off the moon

— Blake Jacobson, 5th grade

DIAMOND

A diamond
has four lines
forming into sharp points
at each edge.
There is nothingness in the middle.
Diamonds are like mirror images
of the peaks of the Rocky Mountains
shimmering
in a lake.
I now
turn my diamond on its side
to make a box
I have a four-sided square now.
A square
is the sight you would see
if you were in a plane
looking down
on a farmer's field of corn.
The Rocky Mountains
surrounded
by a field of corn
The reflection
shimmering in a lake.

— Zachary Howard, 9th grade

HALLOWEEN

With "Halloween," students create a poem about Halloween, focusing on both the experience of the holiday and the season. The resulting poem includes a metaphor that compares a Halloween activity to an aspect of autumn.

PROJECT IDEAS

When illustrated, the "Halloween" poems are perfect for a holiday bulletin board or other public display.

SUGGESTED READINGS

Norton Anthology of Modern Poetry

"Souvenir," Edwin Arlington Robinson, page 222

Piping Down the Valleys Wild

"October Magic," Myra Cohn Livingston, page 64

"Hallowe'en," Harry Behn, page 65

"What Night Would It Be?" John Ciardi, page 66

"The Witches' Ride," Karla Kuskin, page 68

"October," John Updike, page 83

Halloween

For people of all ages, Halloween is often a day full of memories and fun. Think about your own Halloween memories — costumes, parties, pranks, treats, etc. Then use the memories to help you with the word gathering steps below.

Word gathering is an important step in the process of writing a poem. When someone is getting dressed for a special event, he or she might look in the closet and carefully select what to wear. It is easier to make a good selection if there are a lot of clothes to choose from.

In the same way, word gathering gives a poet a lot of choices. He or she looks through all the words, phrases and sentences gathered and makes careful choices for the final poem.

Word Gathering

Step 1: When you think of Halloween, what images come to mind? Brainstorm a list of words.

Examples: *witches, pumpkins, costumes, candy*

Step 2: Imagine yourself on a specific Halloween night from the past. Then make a list of emotions and sensations from that night. Concentrate on your five senses. What did you hear, see, smell, taste? What were you wearing? How did it feel?

Examples: *going to Grandma's house in my mummy costume*
feeling hot and sticky inside the layers of sheets torn into strips

Step 3: Halloween occurs in autumn. Describe autumn. Concentrate on specific details.

Examples: *frosty mornings*
a rainbow of colored leaves on the trees

Step 4: List your favorite Halloween activities and describe each one *objectively.* In other words, tell what is happening without any emotions or feelings or thoughts entering into the description.

Example: Objective description of trick-or-treating — *I walk to the door. I ring the doorbell. I hold out my bag.*

Step 5: Now describe your favorite Halloween activities *subjectively.* In other words, tell about your thoughts, feelings and emotions.

Example: Subjective description of trick or treating — *I hurry to the door, hoping that I'll get Snickers bars instead of apples, worrying about the big kids coming down the block.*

Step 6: Create metaphors that compare your favorite Halloween activities to autumn.

Example: *The sound of eating candy is like the crunching of leaves underfoot.*

Now you are ready to go on to the next stages of writing your poem. See "Extracting a Poem," "Revising" and "Sharing" (pages 135-153).

Pumpkins, candy, costumes.
Night is bright with all the lights.
Red and orange leaves
cover the ground,
crunch under my feet
like candy in my mouth.

— Joylani Ann Leong, 6th grade

Bones rot in graves,
human stench nearby.
Darkness creeps over the horizon,
wails can be heard in the distance,
claws tear.
An icy watery chill in my veins
travels my lower back
to my spinal cortex
giving me a shock.
Doomsday night grows long.
Wind blows cold dry air;
nothing moves.
I hide behind dark corners
as distant hills disappear in low fog.

— Jon Phillip Davis, Jr., 6th grade

when the weather gets colder
and leaves change colors
from a green we've seen all summer
to brilliant scarlets and crisp oranges
and then fall from the trees
to crunch under our feet
you know it's time

when you get used to school
and the first snows come
delighting and exciting us
as we prepare for the upcoming winter
by getting out our jeans
and sweaters colorful as the changing leaves
you know it's time

time for halloween
hot and sticky under itchy costumes
we parade around the streets
getting skittles, snickers, starbursts
from each house along the way.

the world is sugary sweet
as a few crystal snowflakes fall
from a starry October sky
catching in our eyelashes
and landing on our lips
as we go from door to door
house to house
wishing every day could be this sweet

— Annie Mackey, 8th grade

A Fruit or a Vegetable

With "Fruit or a Vegetable," students create a word picture of a fruit or vegetable.

Point out that their poems will probably be more interesting if they choose fruits or vegetables that they either love or hate. Strong feelings often generate strong writing.

You may even want to bring a selection of fruits and vegetables into class for students to choose from. Include interesting and unusual items like jicama, ugli fruit or ginger root.

Project Ideas

"Fruit or Vegetable" poems, with illustrations, can make an attractive and interesting display. Students can draw or paint their fruits and vegetables, or they can make collages of pictures cut from magazines. A local supermarket or grocery store might even be interested in displaying your students' work.

Suggested Readings

Norton Anthology of Modern Poetry

"Study of Two Pears," Wallace Stevens, page 295

"The Tropics in New York," Claude McKay, page 517

Piping Down the Valleys Wild

"City Traffic," Eve Merriam, page 190

A Fruit or a Vegetable

Do you wonder how anyone can even look at cauliflower, much less eat it? Do you love green apples but hate green beans? How do you feel about eggplant?

Choose a fruit or vegetable that interests you, for whatever reason. Now write a poem about it. Begin by following the word gathering steps below.

Think about your attitude toward the fruit or vegetable you have chosen. As you write, try to choose words that show that attitude. You may be surprised at how something as ordinary as a vegetable will actually take on personality in your poem.

Write as much as possible. Don't worry about being sensible. Be creative. Be different. Try every step, but remember that you don't have to use something from every step in your final poem.

Word Gathering

Step 1: Describe the color of your fruit or vegetable. Be creative. You might create a simile in your description. You might choose to mix up your senses and tell what a color "smells" like, "sounds" like, "feels" like or "tastes" like.

Examples: *The color of broccoli is like mold on a crust of bread.*
The color of broccoli smells like dirty socks.

Step 2: Create a story that briefly explains why the fruit or vegetable is the color it is.

Example: *Broccoli used to be cauliflower, until one day a farmer's fairy godmother dropped some into a vat of melted grass clippings. She liked the look.*

Step 3: Characterize the fruit or vegetable as a certain "type" of person or group of people.

Example: *Broccoli is a punk rock group.*

Step 4: Compare the fruit or vegetable to a time of year.

Example: *Broccoli is as green as a July meadow.*

Step 5: Describe how the fruit or vegetable is like you. What do you have in common? Make comparisons of personality traits, physical characteristics, similar experiences, etc.

Example: *I can be as obnoxious as broccoli, and I smell just as bad after I've spent an afternoon playing soccer.*

Step 6: If the fruit or vegetable could talk, what would it say?

Example: *Broccoli might say, "Don't bind me with those little rubber bands in the supermarket!"*

(Optional)
Step 7: Complete the following sentence: "People should know this about (the fruit or vegetable) . . ."

Example: *People should know that broccoli may destroy your taste buds forever.*

(Optional)
Step 8: List traits that the fruit or vegetable is *not.*

Example: *Broccoli is neither sweet nor polite.*

Now you are ready to go on to the next stages of writing your poem. See "Extracting a Poem," "Revising" and "Sharing" (pages 135-153).

The color of crookneck squash
is like the boring yellow
of the original post-it notes,
and it reminds me of the sound
of messages I'd rather not hear.
The crookneck is timid,
and a bit of a coward,
always bending back
to look where it has already been.
The crookneck is the first week of
summer, like the first warm day
when I take my blouse off with skin
still pale.
The crookneck loves the earth,
and stays close to the ground;
it does not need to stoop like me
to discover the simple truths of nature.
The crookneck is misunderstood:
it is not bent, but curved
in an attempt to embrace.
People should know this about
crooknecks:
for squash they are actually bold —
compare them to their cousins,
the zucchini.
They are definitely not green
with envy
or from lack of experience.
This is not a chiropractor poem.
This is not a poem about crime.
This is not a poem about having
to go to posture class.
This is not a poem about loneliness.
This is a poem about love
not girl meets boy,
but it is a love poem . . .

— Kelly Figme, 9th grade

YAMS

Denver Bronco orange,
tangy,
brown-sugar.
Bloated stomach feeling
screaming cousins
blaring TV
Detroit Lions —
always on Thanksgiving.
Rusty potatoes and marshmallow creme
mixed together,
sweet like my Grandma,
and just as old
looking,
like Uncle Bob
without his dentures.
Pigskin leathery outside,
buttery and rich inside.

What are these
rotten
November
potatoes?

— Chris Markuson, college

Favorite Activity

With "Favorite Activity," students describe a favorite activity and, at the same time, take a closer look at themselves.

Before you begin, it's a good idea to spend some time helping students think of activities. You might even want to brainstorm a list of activities with the group — playing volleyball, building model airplanes, talking on the telephone, etc. Point out that even the most ordinary activities can be the subjects of interesting poems. Similarly, very interesting activities can be the subject of very boring poems. It all depends upon the words chosen.

Another subject you might want to address is rhyme. Many of the poems in the "Suggested Readings" are rhymed poems. That doesn't mean that the students' poems should rhyme. In fact, rhyme is usually something new poets should not attempt right away, until they are more familiar with other elements of a poem.

Project Ideas

If you are pleased with the "Favorite Activity" poems your students create, you might have the poems displayed at appropriate places around town. Ask a ski shop to display the poems about skiing, a library to display poems about reading, a kitchen store to display poems about cooking. You might also ask students to add illustrations or photographs to their creations.

Suggested Readings

Norton Anthology of Modern Poetry

"Birches," Robert Frost, page 249

"The Fish," Elizabeth Bishop, page 820

"Diving into the Wreck," Adrienne Rich, page 1327

"Getting in the Wood," Gary Snyder, page 1391

"Inner Tube," Michael Ondaatje, page 1603

Piping Down the Valleys Wild

"Tiptoe," Karla Kuskin, page 3

"Every Time I Climb a Tree," David McCord, page 4

"The Swing," Robert Louis Stevenson, page 5

"Kite," David McCord, page 7

"Flying," Kaye Starbird, page 16

Favorite Activity

Any activity can make an interesting poem, if you concentrate on including interesting details and powerful verbs. To create a "Favorite Activity" poem, first choose a subject. Pick something that you like to do. It could be something active, like playing basketball in the driveway, or something quiet, like reading a magazine in bed. Whatever you choose, try to let the reader know what makes this activity enjoyable to you.

Begin by completing the word gathering steps below. Concentrate on choosing colorful words and interesting details. Remember that word gathering helps you collect ideas and phrases for your final poem.

Try to think of interesting, specific words and phrases. For example, instead of describing something as "enjoyable," say that it was "thrilling" or "A-plus" or "full of smiles." Instead of writing that you "went" somewhere, say that you "raced" or "shuffled" or "bounced." Choosing the best words now will later help you create a poem that is interesting and alive.

Word Gathering

Step 1: Describe your favorite activity. Include one simile or metaphor in your description.

Example: *Playing the piano is like riding to another universe on beams of light.*

Step 2: Imagine you are "doing" the activity. Describe what you are doing objectively. In other words, just give the facts. Tell what your various body parts are doing, using active verbs.

Examples: *My hands curve over the piano keyboard.*
My wrists rise higher than my fingers.
My back lines up straight.

Step 3: Describe how you feel as you do this activity. What are you thinking? Why is it your favorite activity?

Examples: *I think about twirling and swirling in the air and traveling to Saturn and Jupiter.*
I love to play because I transform myself into someone else when I start the music.

Step 4: Describe how your favorite activity ends.

Example: *When my mother calls me for dinner, I have to return to reality.*

Step 5: Finish the poem by describing what you normally do at the end of your favorite activity.

Example: *I stand up and stretch like a cat in the sun. Then I shake my hands until my arms feel loose.*

Now you are ready to go on to the next stages of writing your poem. See "Extracting a Poem," "Revising" and "Sharing" (pages 135-153).

BASKETBALL

Basketball is my shrink.
Whether to swat it away
or to run with it
slam it down
to the earth.

Smooth leather caresses my fingertips.
The ball passes through my legs
in a poetic motion.
They know the game is won when
I flick my wrists.
The silent swoosh
hushes the boos.

When I play I'm an
impenetrable fortress.
I'm untouchable
sitting alone on my cloud
looking down
at the other team.
I
smile.
They can't stop me.
They know that.

There is no end to my game.
I'll never stop
until I'm dead.
My ashes will be
in a basketball urn.

When the game is over
and I know I've won
or done my best,
I make sure not to gloat.
That's for when I'm telling my grandchildren.
And if I lose,
I don't cry in their presence.
I save that for a reason to go back
and practice another couple
of hours.

— Carlos Giron, high school

SAXOPHONE

Playing the saxophone
is like
re-energizing
the music of Charlie Parker,
Clarence Clemmons
and Lisa Simpson
just
by blowing
in a brass tube
with holes in it.
My fingers
fly
over the keys.
As I wail
on my sax,
I feel like I'm in a recording studio
performing the greatest sounds
that ever came out of a horn.
Then I stop
and reality settles in.
I put it away
and wander out of my room.
My sax
lounges there
waiting for me
to start it up again.

— Zachary Howard, 9th grade

FOUR SEASONS

With "Four Seasons," students create a poem about the four seasons of the year, capturing their own experiences with the changes in the yearly cycle.

Note that students write the "Four Seasons" poem in four parts, using the same steps for each season. Have them start with winter, go to spring and summer and end with fall.

PROJECT IDEAS

Students often enjoy adding illustrations to their poems, creating a unique calendar. The easiest approach is to make the kind of calendar that shows all the months of the year at a glance.

Another idea is to divide the class members into groups by their favorite (or least favorite) season. Then have each group compose a stanza about the season it has chosen. Put the four stanzas together into a class poem about the four seasons of the year.

SUGGESTED READINGS

Norton Anthology of Modern Poetry

"The Wood-Pile," Robert Frost, page 246

"The Snow Man," Wallace Stevens, page 289

"November Cotton Flower," Jean Toomer, page 564

"Year's End," William Everson, page 846

"Poem in October," Dylan Thomas, page 922

"The Trees," Philip Larkin, page 1065

"Snow Signs," Charles Tomlinson, page 1247

"Snowfall: A Poem About Spring," James Wright, page 1292

"Stray Animals," James Tate, page 1606

"In Cold Storm Light," Leslie Marmon Silko, page 1648

Piping Down the Valleys Wild

"On a Snowy Day," Dorothy Aldis, page 42

"Snow in Spring," Ivy O. Eastwick, page 43

"Snow Toward Evening," Melville Cane, page 44

"A Summer Morning," Rachel Field, page 48

"April," Sara Teasdale, page 81

"January," John Updike, page 90

Four Seasons

How do you feel about the different seasons of the year? Do you love the whiteness of winter, or are you more fond of the sunshine of summer? Is there a season you dislike? Is there one that is a favorite? Do you like them all equally?

Whatever your feelings, try to make them apparent in the poem you will be creating — but without coming right out and saying how you feel. For example, if you really enjoy summer, you might describe the sun as "warming you into sweet daydreams." If you hate summer, you might describe the sun as "harsh rays beating on your skin like an over-ambitious drummer."

Although you will be writing a poem that includes all four seasons of the year, look at the seasons one at a time. First follow the word gathering steps below for winter. Start over and do them for spring, then summer, then fall.

Since every season has lots of images associated with it, allow yourself plenty of paper to get all your ideas down. Remember that word gathering is just the first step in writing a poem. You will be selecting bits and pieces of your ideas for a final poem about the four seasons.

Word Gathering

Season

Step 1: Think about winter. Write a general description of the season, concentrating on the sights and sounds of the weather. What does winter look like? What does it sound like? Try to use words that show your attitude about the subject.

Examples: *Winter is quiet and still and peaceful. The snow softens everything.*
A gentle snowstorm settles calmly over the meadow.

Step 2: Now look at the general description you have just written. Narrow your focus and add details. For example, if you mentioned *a gentle snowstorm*, narrow your focus to add details about a gentle snowstorm.

Example: *snowflakes falling softly onto the stillness of a frozen lake*

Step 3: Imagine a person (it may or may not be you) or an animal in the scene you have created. Describe this character or animal. What is he/she/it doing?

Example: *A smiling four-year-old boy holds his dad's hand as they climb through the snowdrifts around the lake.*

Step 4: Describe a mood associated with the scene you have created. What is the person or animal feeling or thinking?

Example: *This little boy feels excited to see snow for the first time in his life.*
He feels safe and happy with his dad.

Go back and complete the four word gathering steps for spring, summer and fall.

Then go on to the next stages of writing your poem. See "Extracting a Poem," "Revising" and "Sharing" (pages 135-153).

FOUR SEASONS

Stiff unthawed people
in straight-jacket coats
scrape icy windows
half-dead engines
screech emptily
browning the snow
when they finally
drive down
glacier streets.

Quick chill in sunlight
shiver of green
coming to life
slight tremor
ground breaks
with blooms
sky breaks
with rain
as a toddler runs
with a kite.

Summer runs in laughing
on a Coppertone wave
plays barefoot on the beach
salt on its lips
berries and melons
on mine
the sun smiles

Oranges and yellows
crackle on the ground
like football fans
in cinnamon stands
pumpkin patched days
and squashy nights
draw the year to a close.

— Amy Rider, college

I hear the wood in the fire burning.
White drops of snow fall from the sky.
I feel the warmth from the fire.
I lay down, and fall asleep.

I love warm earthquake weather
with no clouds in the sky.
I play basketball:
release a three, and as I see it miss,
I wonder what I did wrong.

My skin is burning.
The sun is at its best.
I walk down California Avenue
with my dog.
I wonder what he is thinking.

The sun is like a California poppy.
I can barely see the moon.
I lie there, staring at the air.
I wonder how far away the sky is.

— Adam Dikeman, 6th grade

FIVE W'S AND AN H

With "Five W's and an H," students create a simple six-line poem by answering these questions: Who? What? Where? When? Why? How?

Spend some time helping students brainstorm ideas for the "who" (or subject) of their poems. Suggest that subjects they know well will make the best poems. For example, it is generally easier for someone to write a poem about her dog Ginger than about the prime minister of England. That's because she probably knows her dog a lot better than she knows the prime minister.

Another idea is to give everyone two minutes to write down as many subjects as possible. Then ask volunteers to share some of their ideas with the class. Hearing other people's ideas will give most students new ideas of their own.

Before students begin their word gathering, it is helpful to have them make a chart like the one below. The chart will help them keep track of their responses.

Who?	**What?**	**How?**	**Where?**	**When?**	**Why?**
Who is the subject of your poem?	What does your "who" do?	Describe how your "who" does each "what."	Describe the location or place where your "who" does each "what."	Describe the time your "who" does each "what."	Describe why you think your "who" does each "what."

Another idea is to use "Five W's and an H" to create a group poem on a subject the class is currently studying. If the class is studying dinosaurs, the group might compose a poem about Tyrannosaurus rex. The "Five W's and an H" questions will help students to review their knowledge. The questions will also give the teacher an indication of how much students have really learned about the subject.

SUGGESTED READINGS

Norton Anthology of Modern Poetry

"The Red Wheelbarrow," William Carlos Williams, page 318

"Flowers by the Sea," William Carlos Williams, page 321

"The Fish," Marianne Moore, page 456

"Reapers," Jean Toomer, page 563

"A Young Girl with a Pitcher Full of Water," David Wagoner, page 1230

Piping Down the Valleys Wild

"The Night," Myra Cohn Livingston, page 54

"Poem," William Carlos Williams, page 114

"Whispers," Myra Cohn Livingston, page 220

Five W's and an H

While you write your "Five W's and an H" poem, think of yourself as a newspaper reporter. Newspaper reporters always answer six questions when they are writing a story: Who? What? Where? When? Why? How?

For your poem, you first need to answer the question "Who?" In other words, choose a subject for your poem. The subject might be a person, like your grandmother. It might be an animal, like your puppy. It might be something from nature, like an ocean wave. It might be an inanimate object, like an alarm clock, a bicycle, your bathroom mirror or the mouse on your computer.

If you pick an inanimate object, you will probably need to personify it. "Personify" means to make the object think, feel or look like a person. For example, you might say, "The mirror stares back at me, bored to death." Mirrors don't *really* stare, and they don't *really* get bored. By using such a description, you are "personifying" the mirror.

As you follow the word gathering steps below, let your imagination go wild. Stretch your brain. Stretch your thinking. Have some fun collecting words, phrases and sentences. You will use them later in composing your poem.

Word Gathering

Step 1: What activities does your "who" perform? Create a list of verbs or action words that describe what your subject does. You may use single words, phrases or both.

Examples: *My cat Katy Kitty purrs*
nibbles at her Fancy Feast
walks on my face when I am sleeping

Step 2: Describe how your "who" performs each activity in Step 1. Use adverbs, similes and metaphors.

Examples: *purrs like a miniature locomotive engine*
nibbles daintily

Step 3: List places where this "who" performs each activity.

Examples: *purrs while she basks in the warm sun*
nibbles as she stands in the laundry room by her pink dish

Step 4: Describe when this "who" performs each activity.

Examples: *purrs in the morning*
nibbles at her food while I eat my own supper

Step 5: List the reasons why this "who" performs each activity.

Examples: *purrs because she is happy and warm*
nibbles at her food because it wouldn't be ladylike to gobble

Now you are ready to go on to the next stages of writing your poem. See "Extracting a Poem," "Revising" and "Sharing" (pages 135-153).

The ocean
dances
on light feet with the quick wind
creating movement
in the peaceful night.
Under the watchful moonlit sky
I realize how small I really am.

— Karis C. Triska, 6th grade

My alarm clock
buzzes, pulses, annoys
ruthless authoritarian
nestled on my nightstand
never flinching
when I pound it
at 7 a.m.

— Amy Rider, college

The wind
gusts and howls
with fury
on the ocean
as evening crashes down
summoning memories of ships lost at sea.

— Tamima Leanna Woods, 6th grade

PETS

With "Pets," students write about their relationship with a favorite pet. For students who don't have a pet, suggest that they write about any animal they have known well — perhaps a former pet or a friend's pet. Another possibility is to have these students do an alternative assignment from this book, perhaps "Animals." (See page 83.)

PROJECT IDEAS

You might try having students write their poems during National Pet Week, which is always the first full week of May. You might also have them make "poem posters," including photographs or drawings of their pets. These could be displayed at pet stores or veterinary clinics.

SUGGESTED READINGS

Norton Anthology of Modern Poetry

"Sandra: At the Beaver Trap," Michael Harper, page 1498

"Biography," Michael Ondaatje, page 1597

Piping Down the Valleys Wild

"The Hairy Dog," Herbert Asquith, page 107

"Lone Dog," Irene Rutherford McLeod, page 108

"Moon," William Jay Smith, page 112

"A gigantic beauty," Walt Whitman, page 124

"The Runaway," Robert Frost, page 125

PETS

Imagine a favorite pet — either one you have now or one you had in the past. Think about that animal. Picture it clearly in your mind.

Then complete the word gathering steps below. As you complete the steps, you will be gathering words, phrases and sentences about your pet. Remember, you won't be writing a poem as you complete these steps. You will be collecting material to use *later* in writing your poem.

Try to avoid clichés as you write. Clichés are those tired, worn-out phrases that you hear all the time. "Quiet as a mouse" is one. If you want to describe "quiet," try to come up with something original, like "quiet as a piece of cottonwood fluff falling in a pool of rainwater."

WORD GATHERING

Step 1: Describe your pet's physical appearance. What are its distinguishing and most lovable characteristics? Include at least one simile or metaphor in the description.

Examples: *My dog Daisy —*
blonde, medium-sized mutt
eyelashes as long and dark as a movie star's
loves everybody and everything, even cats

Step 2: Describe yourself, from your pet's perspective. How do you think your pet sees you?

Example: *Daisy thinks of me as another breed of dog — one that's taller and a little smarter than her.*

Step 3: What do you have in common with your pet? What about you is different? Compare physical traits, personality traits, experiences, etc.

Examples: *both nervous and antsy and blonde*
I am skinny, but she is round and puffy.

Step 4: What have you learned from your pet? How is your life different because of the animal?

Examples: *I've learned how nice it is to have someone just accept me, no matter what.*
I know I always have someone to listen to me.

Now you are ready to go on to the next stages of writing your poem. See "Extracting a Poem," "Revising" and "Sharing" (pages 135-153).

BUZZ

Reddish-brown bear in disguise,
this puppy hikes
three for my every one mile —
sniffing air and redwood bark,
chasing butterflies,
roughing grass and blackberry bush,
an occasional lizard tail in mouth.

Attentive to me, he watches
how far I am lumbering behind,
sees the runt of the litter
slowly climb the steep slopes
or the snow-covered ones
that he so playfully romps.
At times, he teases — running off,
both of us temporarily lost.

Buzz and I play so differently:
I focus on the distant lake;
his eyes scan the immediate ground.
But we have a symbiotic relationship;
I walk on knowing he blazes the trail;
he waits smelling reward in my hand.
Together we manage to journey
there and home.

— Kelly Figme, 9th grade

ANN

A pint-sized kitten with
out of place patches of peach,
a 5-year old on a sugar high.

I'm her guardian, hero
mother,
constantly nagging her, shielding out trouble.

We are soul mates, wild and curious,
intimidated by a world where
age = knowledge
and knowledge = power

She is my best friend —
a caring face in a
cruel world.

— Carlos Giron, high school

Brothers and Sisters

With "Brothers and Sisters," students write about their relationship with a brother or sister. If a student is an only child, encourage him or her to write about any relative, or even a very close friend.

Suggested Readings

Norton Anthology of Modern Poetry

"Lost Sister," Cathy Song, page 1736

BROTHERS AND SISTERS

Writing a poem about a brother or a sister is sometimes easier than writing other poems. That's because, when it comes to siblings, most of us have strong feelings, both good and bad. Also, brothers and sisters are usually people we know pretty well, and it's always easier to write about a subject we know well.

Choose one of your brothers or sisters as the subject for your poem. If you don't have any siblings, try choosing any relative or a close friend — anyone you know well. Then begin the word gathering steps below.

As you complete the steps, include as many details as possible. Describe your brother's wiry head of red hair or the annoying way he picks his teeth at the table. Mention the way he surprised you with a little hug that time you were in so much trouble with your parents. In other words, be as specific as possible.

Remember that word gathering is the first step in creating your poem. Collecting details ahead of time will help you create an interesting, vivid poem.

WORD GATHERING

Step 1: Compare yourself to your brother or sister (or to the person you have chosen as the subject of your poem). Compare the two of you physically — age, size, hair color, eye color, etc. Also compare personality traits, moods, emotions, goals, etc. Tell how you are similar and how you are different.

Examples: *My sister has black hair, and so do I.*
My sister is shy, but I am outgoing.

Step 2: List some activities that you enjoy doing together.

Examples: *going to the movies*
baking cookies
playing tennis

Step 3: Describe in detail one typical activity. Try to choose an activity that shows something important about the relationship between the two of you. For example, a description of shooting baskets might show how competitive you are. A description of helping your little sister buy some new shoes might show how much she looks up to you.

Examples: *She picks up each pair of shoes and then looks at me.*
waits for my smile or frown
gets enthusiastic if I like a pair, too

Step 4: List activities that you do *not* enjoy doing together. List typical arguments.

Examples: *doing dishes*
arguing about whose turn it is to empty the dishwasher
She hates it if I don't make all the silverware face the same way in the basket.

Step 5: Create a simile or metaphor that compares the relationship between the two of you to something in nature.

Examples: *Our relationship is unpredictable, like the weather.*
I am a mother cat and she is a kitten watching every move I make.

Step 6: What do you like about your brother or sister? What does he/she like about you?

Examples: *I like the way she almost always wants to do what I want to do.*
She likes the way I stick up for her.

Step 7: What do you dislike about your brother or sister? What does he/she dislike about you?

Examples: *I hate the way she eats the soft middles of French bread and then puts jelly on all the crusts and eats them separately.*
She hates the way I don't listen.

Step 8: How do you imagine your relationship will be in the future? How would you like it to be?

Examples: *I think we will always live in the same town.*
I want her to keep asking for my advice forever.

Now you are ready to go on to the next stages of writing your poem. See "Extracting a Poem," "Revising" and "Sharing" (pages 135-153).

THE BROTHER POEM

My brother is seven and active.
I am eleven and patient.
We argue about where we sit in the car.
We read together on the couch.
He reads me short books.
I read him stories and fables.
I like his sense of humor.
He likes the way I play Monopoly with him.
I hope our relationship gets better.
We are like a river,
mostly rushing and roaring,
but sometimes calm and peaceful.

— Casey Lurtz, 5th grade

FEELING LIKE SISTERS

I've always wanted to work with wild animals.
Melissa wants to be an artist.
I have blue eyes like the sky.
Melissa has brown eyes like a cave.
Melissa and I love to go places to see guys.
We love to go shopping so we can ask
each other questions about what to buy.
My sister and I hate to play games
with each other
because we accuse the other of cheating.
I think life is important,
if you use it wisely.
She thinks being smooth
in front of guys is cool.
I thought that saying "hi"
to someone I didn't know was nice,
but she thinks it's embarrassing.
I'm the flash of roaring lightning;
she is the quiet, motionless tree.
I think we will be closer together
when we get older,
and that we need to fight now
or we wouldn't feel like sisters.

— Melody Michael Lovato, 5th grade

I'm older
and taller
my hair is lighter
and longer

She has brown eyes
and curlier hair
her knees have more scars
and she has bangs

I'm outgoing
and more laid back
I'm super friendly
and my goals change frequently

she's shy
but hyper
she's hard to get to know
and sticks to her goals

we like volleyball
and basketball
baking cookies
and rollerblading

we fight about chores
and who does more
I do chores faster
and she does a better job

we are a pair
like thunder and lightening
moon and stars
sunshine and rainbows

she always laughs
at my stupid jokes
I always let her
borrow my clothes

it bothers me
how slow she eats
she hates the way
I eat so fast

I hope we can always be friends
and she will always ask my advice
because despite our differences
I still love her

— Annie Mackey, 8th grade

How-To

With "How-To," students describe how to perform a certain task. The choice of tasks is up to them. However, it is a good idea to point out that poems can be more interesting when they involve less practical subjects. A poem about how to fix a washing machine is often less interesting than a poem about a more spiritual, emotional or philosophical topic, like how to save your soul, how to stay alive in the woods or how to make a friend.

Encourage students to be creative in choosing topics for their how-to poems. You might even suggest that they explore roles, with subjects like "How to Be a Seventh Grader," "How to Be a Sister," "How to Be a Parent" or "How to Be a Teacher."

Suggested Readings

Norton Anthology of Modern Poetry

"Diving into the Wreck," Adrienne Rich, page 1327

"Meeting the Mountains," Gary Snyder, page 1390

"Cleaning a Fish," Dave Smith, page 1580

Piping Down the Valleys Wild

"Going to Bed," Marchette Chute, page 20

"I'll Tell You How," Emily Dickinson, page 47

How-To

With a "How-To" poem, you tell how to do something. It can be something practical, like "how to snowboard" or "how to mow a lawn." It can be something less concrete, like "how to be popular" or "how to be a good sport."

Choose a subject that interests you. Then imagine actually doing the task. What are the important actions to remember?

Follow the word gathering steps below to get started. Since word gathering is an "anything goes" stage, don't censor yourself. Write down everything that comes to mind as you go through the steps. You may be surprised at how much you come up with, so be sure you have lots of paper.

Word Gathering

Step 1: What exactly are you going to describe how to do? Be specific and complete.

Example: *how to make a baby laugh*

Step 2: Lay out the directions for how to accomplish your task, step by step. Start at the beginning and tell what to do next, and then next. Be sure to explain the desired results of each step. Also tell us what to think and feel as we complete each step.

Example: *Get the baby's attention by standing right in front of him and saying his name. (The baby should look at you then. You will know you are on the right track.) Looking at the baby, back up until you are hidden from the baby's view. (The baby should be watching you as you back off. Feel happy that you have his attention.)*

Step 3: Create a setting or place for your task. Where could the task be taking place? Describe the setting.

Example: *on the floor in front of a sofa, with the baby on a blanket*

Step 4: Go back to your step-by-step directions from Step 2. Connect certain steps in performing the task to your setting.

Example: *Back up until you are behind the arm of the sofa, hidden from the baby's view.*

Step 5: What is this activity like? Create several metaphors and similes to describe it.

Examples: *Making a baby laugh is as much fun as eating mocha chip ice cream sprinkled with M & M's.*
Making a baby laugh is like being the star of a hit movie.

Step 6: What are the results of your activity? What lessons do you learn?

Examples: *Giggles*
Legs kicking excitedly into the air
If only I could make everyone happy by doing so little.

Now you are ready to go on to the next stages of writing your poem. See "Extracting a Poem," "Revising" and "Sharing" (pages 135-153).

shopping really clears your head
you gain clothes
and a sense of accomplishment
I recommend it to anyone feeling bummed
or broken hearted

first you select a person who can go for a long time
call them up and ask what they're wearing
select a time and place to meet
food courts are the best place to meet
wear good shoes

strategically plan where to go
and how to get there
to ensure maximum shopping
in minimal time
walk fast

the first time around just look
pick stuff out that you like
after you see everything
go back around
this time to buy

try on the things you picked out
get your partner's opinion
buy it if you decide you need it
ask a few times if they really like what you bought
but know inside that they do

repeat this until
a) time runs out
b) money runs out
c) energy runs out
be sure to take a few breaks

shopping is like a long clear waterfall
a sweet piece of fruit
you feel so clean inside
and closer to the person you went with
shopping is so cool

— Annie Mackey, 8th grade

HOW TO LOVE JULY

Buy fireworks and Slurpees
never wear shoes
but sunglasses instead
Rock on a porch swing
Sing "Dock of the Bay"
at the beach
Go to a fair
Have breakfast outside
and plant radishes
Drink sun tea with a slice
of orange
Swimming every day
and night
your sister braids
your hair
And from a swinging
hammock watch the fireflies
watch you.

— Amy Rider, college

With "Animals," students write a poem about an animal, doing research about the animal in order to depict it accurately.

Research should be guided by the prompts in the word gathering steps. It's a good idea to have encyclopedias, books and periodicals available in the classroom for research, or allow time in the library.

If the class has been studying an animal in class, you might have the students create a group poem about the animal. Simply lead the class as a whole through the word gathering steps, writing responses on the black board or the overhead projector. Then have students choose words and phrases to compose a poem.

Project Ideas

If illustrated, the animal poems lend themselves to the creation of a class "bestiary" suitable for bulletin boards or other public display.

Suggested Readings

Norton Anthology of Modern Poetry

"The Fish," Marianne Moore, page 456

"The Wellfleet Whale," Stanley Kunitz, page 706

"White Oxen," Louis Simpson, page 1104

"The Horses," Ted Hughes, page 1395

"Roe Deer," Ted Hughes, page 1402

Piping Down the Valleys Wild

"The Owl," William Jay Smith, page 134

"Something Told the Wild Geese," Rachel Field, page 135

"The Heron," Theodore Roethke, page 137

"Bee Song," Carl Sandburg, page 143

"Mrs. Spider," Myra Cohn Livingston, page 146

"The Bat," Theodore Roethke, page 147

"Four Little Foxes," Lew Sarett, page 150

"All But Blind," Walter de la Mare, page 152

"The Black Snake," Patricia Hubbell, page 154

Animals

Poetry involves looking at the world in different ways — some might even say with "new eyes." As you create a poem about an animal, try to think of new and interesting ways to describe it.

For example, you may learn from an encyclopedia that a small perch weighs 12 ounces. In your poem, you might say that a perch "weighs about as much as a can of Mountain Dew."

After you have selected the animal you want to write about, follow the word gathering steps below. When you need more information in order to answer questions, do some research. Go to encyclopedias, science text-books, the Internet or other sources.

As you complete the steps, let yourself go. Be creative. Have some fun playing with language. You will use the words and phrases you gather when you start composing your final poem.

Word Gathering

Step 1: What animal have you chosen? Where does it live? Describe its habitat.

Example: *turtle*
rocks and reeds of a pond or lake

Step 2: Describe the animal: size, shape, color, weight, texture, etc. The encyclopedia is a good source for this information.

Example: *the size of a heavy loaf of bread*
dried hard on the outside but soft underneath

Step 3: How is the animal like you? What do you have in common? Make comparisons. You might consider personality traits, physical characteristics, experiences, etc.

Example: *We both like to bask in the summer sun and hide from winter.*

Step 4: If you were the animal, what could you do with its abilities?

Example: *I'd pull my head inside my shell whenever I was embarrassed.*

Step 5: If the animal were a "kind" of weather, what would it be?

Example: *A turtle's shell is like hard pellets of hail covering the ground.*

Step 6: List some facts you have discovered about your animal. You might even want to include its scientific name.

Example: *Sea turtle oil has been used for centuries for lotions, medicines and cosmetic products.*
Lepiochelys kempil

(Optional)
Step 7: Briefly tell a myth or legend about your animal.

Example: *Turtle threw a party in the sky and fell to make the earth. (From a Native American myth.)*

(Optional)
Step 8: Tell the animal's collective name.

Examples: *a bale of turtles*
a herd of bison
a flock of seagulls
a gaggle of geese

Now you are ready to go on to the next stages of writing your poem. See "Extracting a Poem," "Revising" and "Sharing" (pages 135-153).

THE DEER

High up in the brush
in the forested glades,
a white-tailed deer.

Slender legs
arching neck
coarse-grained
nut-brown pelt.

Fleet
leaping gracefully,
quick as lightning,
light as the air,
it eludes the hunters

— Tamima Leanna Woods, 6th grade

SCORPIONS

Scorpions
quietly run over the sand
in the hot, dry desert.
When born, they are alive,
and cling to their mothers' backs.
Small, red, poisonous,
and built like a tank.
Watch your step:
its sting is like a heatwave of
pain!

— Jacob Meng, 6th grade

WILD HORSES

Unlike your tame ancestors,
you are wild, like a hurricane,
with the need to run free

white and golden flecks
on a grassy prairie
a herd of mustangs

— Risa Strobel, 6th grade

MUSIC

With "Music," students gain an understanding of a piece of music by learning how to listen. Then they translate their understanding to words.

Before class, choose a piece of instrumental music to play for the group. Any of thousands of recordings will work well. You might consider jazz, classical, new age, ragtime, heavy metal, or ethnic music, to name just a few.

Play your selection once for the class before students begin the word gathering steps. Then play it again for Steps 3-5 and again for Step 6.

Another idea is to have the class write a group poem, basing it on a musical composition from a time period the class is currently studying.

Music

Writing a poem about a specific piece of music can be challenging and fun. First, of course, you need to hear the music. Try closing your eyes and letting your imagination run wild as you listen.

After you listen to the music, you are ready to begin the word gathering steps below. Remember that word gathering involves gathering words, phrases and ideas for your poem. Write down thoughts and ideas that randomly pop into your head when you hear the music. Don't worry about being "right" or "correct." Poetry allows you to break rules and look at the world in new and different ways.

Word Gathering

Step 1: Describe the general tone and mood of the music. How does it make you feel? This requires only one or two words.

Example: *laid back, relaxed*
nostalgic

Step 2: Describe what the notes "do." Compare that "doing" to an action that occurs in nature.

Example: *Notes climb the scale like spiders scurrying up a wall.*

Step 3: What does the music make you feel like doing?

Example: *swaying and dancing and sipping iced tea in the heat*

Step 4: Where would you like to do the activity from Step 3? Describe the setting. Use words that will help create a scene.

Example: *dancing outside at the church bazaar in July*
The smell of tamales and green chile waltz in the air around the asphalt parking lot lit with tiny white bulbs strung from pole to pole.

Step 5: Choose one part of your body and describe what it does when you are engaged in the activity from Step 3.

Example: *My head starts swaying gently to the beat.*

Step 6: What does the music sound like? Are the sounds fat or thin? Big or small? What shape are they? What is their texture? Describe them. To make your poem consistent, choose sounds that might originate in the setting you described in Step 4.

Example: *The sounds are so smooth and cool they clash with the hot rough dance floor.*

Now you are ready to go on to the next stages of writing your poem. See "Extracting a Poem," "Revising" and "Sharing" (pages 135-153).

MUSIC

Calm
Tired
The notes flow
Like a wave rolling
across the ocean.
I feel like taking a nap
or just
looking out the window.
From my living room
the moon shines in
from the sky.
My eyes shut
and I see brilliant
colors flow along
with the mood of
the music.
The sounds
are then
smooth and soft
like the moon
casting a gentle
glow
on the
surroundings.

— Zachary Howard, 9th grade

I look into
the deep, dark, black pit of pain.
Black, brown, and navy
colors of anguish swirl in agony.
Crumbling, distortion —
the pit is my home,
and my salvation.

— Erin Sullivan Meyer, 8th grade

Quick notes
fly up the scales
like a redwood growing taller

running through the forest,
damp, cold trees surround me
like the rings of Saturn.
My feet lift, fall;
as I run,
the sweat settles in crannies.

All alone,
with the swift movement of deer,
I run gracefully, blowing in the wind,
I discover life!

— Tibi Girczyc-Blum, 6th grade

MUSIC

The notes sound like a tree
gently swaying in the wind
in the heart of a forest
on a warm spring day;
I stand and listen
to the relaxing sound of the tree.

The music sounds like the ocean
washing back to the shore
on the beach: calm and peaceful;
I walk along the water,
the waves at my feet,
the soft sand in my toes.

— Alexandra Weinstein-Haven, 6th grade

Work of Art

As students write "Work of Art" poems, they also gain an understanding of a piece of visual art by learning how to "see." The poem requires that the viewer identify with the artist and/or a character within the painting.

Before you begin, gather poster-sized reproductions of art work in a wide variety of styles. You might also use art books with large reproductions of paintings. If the class is studying a particular painter or period, you may choose to limit the paintings to that artist or period. All of the selections should depict at least one human character.

The exercise is a good opportunity to explore art history in the classroom.

Suggested Readings

Norton Anthology of Modern Poetry

"In Goya's Greatest Scenes We Seem to See," Lawrence Ferlinghetti, page 1005

"The Starry Night," Anne Sexton, page 1307

"Beauty and Sadness," Cathy Song, page 1735

WORK OF ART

For a poem about a work of art, choose a painting or drawing that you find interesting in some way. (You don't necessarily need to *like* the painting.) Be sure that the painting is one that includes a person in it.

Study your painting closely. Become familiar with it. Imagine what might be happening in the scene depicted.

Then begin the word gathering steps below. You may write words, phrases and/or sentences. At this stage, you don't need to worry about punctuation, grammar, spelling or anything except collecting interesting words and ideas to use later when you begin constructing your poem.

WORD GATHERING

Step 1: The title of your poem will be the title of the painting followed by the artist's name.

Example: *The Flower Seller, by Diego Rivera*

Step 2: Using all your senses, describe the setting or scene so that anyone can imagine it. Include a metaphor in your description. Try to paint the scene in words.

Example: *middle of Mexico City*
too much pollution making everything dirty and grimy
and hot, like the inside of a heated coal stove

Step 3: Describe in detail one character in the painting. What is the person doing, thinking, and feeling? If you had the opportunity to ask this person a question, what would you ask? Break the silence of the artwork with some empathy for this character.

Example: *The young flower seller peddles white calla lilies.*
clean brown hair braided with a white ribbon to match
her white dress
Why are you here? You are too young.
She knows she has to work to live.

Step 4: How does the painting make you feel — sad, happy, thoughtful or what? What in the painting contributes to that feeling?

Example: *I feel worried for her because she looks like she doesn't belong in this scene.*
She looks out of place because she is so clean and everything else is so grimy.

Step 5: If you had the opportunity to ask the artist a question, what would you ask?

Example: *Is the girl real? Could she be an angel?*

Step 6: What does the painting mean to you? What do you think the artist is trying to "say"? What ideas or feelings do you think the artist is trying to express? Remember, there are no right or wrong answers here.

Example: *The artist might be saying that there is always hope and innocence, even in the midst of gloom.*

Now you are ready to go on to the next stages of writing your poem. See "Extracting a Poem," "Revising" and "Sharing" (pages 135-153).

THE EVE OF ST. JOHN,
BY PETER HURD

Darkness creeps its way toward the
small village
sweeping a pitch black blanket across
the sky.
Muffled noises in the starless night,
the white pale moon provided little light.
I look deep into the flame as it dances
around
casting shadows on the valley floor.
Hooves sound behind me.
The flame flickers, I cup my hand over
it.
My candle is the only light to the world,
I must not let it go out.
I stare deep into the flame,
watch it change red orange yellow.
A voice calls from the cabin
I want to run to her, but I must not.
I must stay here.

— Ursula Jansson, 6th grade

THE EVE OF ST. JOHN,
BY PETER HURD

The sun slowly sinks behind the
mountains.
The lights of a far off cabin reflect onto
the field.
The pounding of horse hooves in the
distance
as she walks into the meadow.
The candle she holds is glowing brightly.
She holds out her hand to protect the
flame from the evening breeze.
Looking at her light, feeling a small ray
of hope —
what if I was that girl?
Standing there alone in the field as the
sun sets,
how would I feel?

— Rebekah Hrdina 6th grade

Clothing Memory

With "Clothing Memory," students describe a memory triggered by a piece of clothing.

Ask students ahead of time to choose a piece of clothing that they once owned, or perhaps still own. They might choose an old rag that used to be a favorite sweatshirt, for example.

Point out that they will be writing about a memory associated with the clothing; therefore, they should try to choose an item that has meaning for them. It will be much easier to write about a favorite sweatshirt worn every night for two years than about a white shirt worn only a couple of times on ordinary days and then forgotten. Students may even want to bring the piece of clothing to class.

Clothing Memory

Most of us have had a piece of clothing that we absolutely loved. Choose a piece of clothing you have loved, and write a poem about it.

You might choose the cowboy vest you played with every day as a child and still have tucked away in a drawer. You might choose the soft, well-worn pair of sweat pants hanging in the back of your closet, the T-shirt you always grab right out of the dryer or that special leather jacket you feel so great wearing. Pick an item of clothing that has memories associated with it. If the clothing has meaning for you, it will be easier to write a poem about it.

Follow the steps in the word gathering exercises below. Try to choose interesting verbs and adjectives that will help us *see* your item of clothing and understand why it was (or is) special. You will later be selecting your best words and phrases as you construct your poem. Interesting verbs and adjectives will help you create a much more powerful poem.

Word Gathering

Step 1: Think about the clothing you have chosen, and picture it in your mind. What is it? Describe it briefly.

Example: *brown neoprene waders that fit like a second skin*

Step 2: What activity does it remind you of? What were you doing when you wore it in the past?

Example: *remind me of the pajamas I wore as a kid*
remind me of going fishing with my grandpa

Step 3: Describe the cloth the clothing is made from. Focus on texture. Include at least one simile or metaphor in your description.

Example: *Neoprene is rough when dry, slimy smooth when wet.*
It feels like the smooth scales of a wild trout.

Step 4: When you were wearing the clothing and engaging in the activity described in Step 2, what would be your typical mood? Describe it. What would the weather typically be? Describe it.

Example: *I was too young to fish, but still I tried to keep up with the pace grandpa set.*
sodden rain, muddy paths

Step 5: What memory does the activity and/or the clothing trigger? Describe that memory. Use specific details. Be sure to incorporate details about the clothing.

Example: *I remember listening to my grandfather's old rubber waders squeak, and how the new neoprene is quite silent.*

Step 6: Compare who you are now to the memory of who you were in Step 4. Have you changed? If so, how? What are you doing that is similar or different?

Example: *It's been six years since grandpa died. I fish alone now.*

Step 7: What has happened to the piece of clothing? What condition is it in?

Example: *The waders stink of salmon roe.*

Now you are ready to go on to the next stages of writing your poem. See "Extracting a Poem," "Revising" and "Sharing" (pages 135-153).

My jacket is big, red and black,
with an Indiana Hoosiers basketball logo
on it.
It keeps me dry like a big umbrella
and reminds me of the flood last winter.
I remember looking at the cold,
wet black sky.
Water was everywhere,
streaming down our lawn,
covering our yard like a big lake.
I remember stacking hay
to keep the water out of our house,
then treading through the water,
splashing everywhere,
to get to our car,
to evacuate our house . . .
My jacket kept me dry.
Now it is smaller, but looks good as new
waiting in the closet,
ready for a new adventure.

— Nick Newman, 5th grade

When "gooder" was the best
word my blue rubber clogs
were my everything shoes
playing dress-up
making mudpies
swinging my legs
off church pews
Mom was horrified.
Inappropriate
big yellow and hot
pink flower sticker
over each toe
straight from the 70s
my clomping clogs with
their waffled bottoms
made grids in the ground
I made my mark.
sunny days
moony nights
sloshing through puddles
those stickers peeled away
one day.

— Amy Rider, college

Long black mesh basketball shorts.
Black Jordan jersey
covering me like a canvas.
My basketball uniform
proudly knowing I rarely lose a game.
The jersey
long and rough
light and strong like a spider's web.
Determined, dedicated, nervous.
Sun beat down on me like L.A. police
on Rodney King
I can't let it win.
A crowded gym.
My game face.
It smells of 100 sweating athletes.
Time for the championship game.
I'm still nervous.
Determined
Dedicated
The more games I win the calmer I become
The shorts and the jersey look as if they were in battle.
I wear them to games,
only to my wins.

— Carlos Giron, high school

Sense of Place

With "Sense of Place," students explore their relationship to a location or spot, either a natural place or a place made by humans.

Suggested Readings

Norton Anthology of Modern Poetry

"The Snow Lies Sprinkled on the Beach," Robert Bridges, page 110

"Evening Ebb," Robinson Jeffers, page 432

"Rocky Acres," Robert Graves, page 567

"The Cottage Hospital," John Betjeman, page 721

"Childhood's Retreat," Robert Duncan, page 997

"Elegy for a Forest Clear-Cut by the Weyerhaeuser Company," David Wagoner, page 1226

"Two Views of Two Ghost Towns," Charles Tomlinson, page 1245

"Blackberrying," Sylvia Plath, page 1427

"The Spire," Ellen Bryant Voigt, page 1592

"Freeway 280," Lorna Dee Cervantes, page 1728

"Leaving," Cathy Song, page 1734

Sense of Place

Spend some time thinking about places in your life that are special to you. Do you especially like a room in your house, a tree fort in the backyard, a particular campsite in the mountains, your uncle's garage, the gas station on the corner of your block? Choose a place that you can easily picture in your mind, a place that has memories and feelings associated with it. This place will be the subject of your poem.

Then follow the word gathering steps below. Try to concentrate on details, specific details that will help others really picture the place you are describing. Try to create a sense of what the place is like for you by using all five senses in your descriptions.

Remember that word gathering is just the first step in writing a poem — collecting information.

Word Gathering

Step 1: What place have you chosen to write about? Describe it. If it is a natural place, list the land forms, ecosystems, plants, animals, etc. If it is not a natural place, describe the materials it is made of, the contents, the design, the layout, etc.

Example: *my grandparents' kitchen*
white, sunny, a green refrigerator
a table with an aluminum edge

Step 2: What makes the place special? What characteristics set it apart from other places?

Example: *the smells of tomato sauce and smoke mingling in the air*

Step 3: Describe the place as a habitat. What or who lives there — either live or inanimate "beings"? You might make an extensive list, or you might highlight only one or two examples.

Examples: *Grandma and Grandpa, tangy aromas and a tiny black radio all live in the kitchen.*

Step 4: Describe what the occupants of your place *do* there. Choose interesting, descriptive verbs.

Examples: *Grandpa smokes, using the ash tray I made for him at school.*
Grandma sets up the little card table where my cousins and I sit.

Step 5: Write a metaphor to describe the place. What does it resemble? Compare it to a person, a flower, a rock . . . anything.

Example: *The sun peers through the sheer curtains.*
It transforms the kitchen into a golden heaven.

Step 6: Write about what the place means to you. What does it represent or symbolize? What feelings do you associate with it? What emotions? Try to write a statement that expresses your understanding of the place.

Example: *The kitchen is love and tradition and Grandma and Grandpa.*

Now you are ready to go on to the next stages of writing your poem. See "Extracting a Poem," "Revising" and "Sharing" (pages 135-153).

There is a trail that leads to
"the clearcut."
Surrounded by a wall of trees
Where mice dwell and
Where foxes hide under brush,
The trees loom and scrape the clouds,
Look like obsidian spikes jutting out of
the ground.
The place seems to be touched by light.
Or enhanced.

— Peter C. Lisle, 6th grade

RAINFOREST

The misty fog dousing my hair;
far off I can hear the songs of wild birds
flying this way and that.
From a distance there's a call
from the king of the jungle.

A place of peace and quiet,
where everything is beautiful.
Snakes, monkeys, birds and anteaters
roam the ground.
Snakes eat mice,
monkeys eat bugs,
birds eat seeds,
anteaters eat ants.

They roam and play all day
and when it's night,
they get into fights for food.

The rain forest is tough
and bold like a rock.

I feel like it won't be there
when I grow up.

— Bryan Wheeless, 4th grade

Centennial recreation club
is one of my favorite places to be
with red clay tennis courts
an L-shaped pool
a sandy volleyball court
and a kiddie pool
it's a place to meet your friends

take a deep breath through your nose
smells like chlorine and sunscreen
lick your lips
it tastes like Sprite and snickers,
our favorite lunch
close your eyes
you can hear the delighted giggles
of small children
splashes as older kids do cannonballs
off the diving board
the voices of new moms talking
about their experiences with kids
and teen-agers talking about how
it's more fun to go back-to-school shopping
than actually going back to school
look around
see every color of swimsuit imaginable
feel around you
cool green grass
soft terry towels
smooth plastic chairs

come here to swim
play tennis or volleyball
talk and gossip
laugh and make plans
babysit for the member's kids

to me this place means sun, fun and friends

— Annie Mackey, 8th grade

PARENT'S HANDS

With "Parent's Hands," students look at their relationship with a parent or caretaker, often gaining a better understanding of themselves in the process.

Before students begin this exercise, ask them to choose a parent or caretaker to write about. Have them prepare two meaningful questions to ask that person.

It's a good idea to give students some guidance with the questions. Talk about the word "meaningful." Ask them to think of questions that might help them understand or get to know their parents better. A question like "What did you have for breakfast?" is not going to help students gain any understanding. A question like "What did you love to do most when you were my age?" might help a student see a parent in a new way.

Have students ask their questions, write down the answers and bring them to class.

SUGGESTED READINGS

Norton Anthology of Modern Poetry

"My Papa's Waltz," Theodore Roethke, page 778

"Spree," Maxine Kumin, page 1146

"The Man of the House," David Wagoner, page 1225

Parent's Hands

Most of us take people for granted sometimes, especially the people closest to us. One of the nicest things about writing a poem is that it can force us to open our eyes. As we search for words, we *really* look, and we *really* see.

Choose one of your parents, or any other person who is very close to you, for the subject of a poem. Then focus on just one part of that person — his or her hands.

Your teacher has asked you to prepare two meaningful questions to ask the person you have chosen. Be sure to ask your questions and write down the person's answers before completing the word gathering steps below.

As you follow the steps below, write down everything that comes to mind. Collect as many interesting words, phrases, sentences and ideas as possible. Later you will use your collection of words to compose a poem.

Word Gathering

Step 1: Tell who you are going to write about. Describe the person's role in your life.

Example: *my grandfather, who has taken care of me since I was three years old*

Step 2: Imagine that you are looking at the person. What is he or she doing? Describe characteristic poses and mannerisms.

Example: *drinking cup after cup of coffee while he reads every single section of the Sunday newspaper*

Step 3: Narrow the focus to the person's hands. Look at your descriptions from Step 2 and describe what the person's hands are doing during these activities.

Example: *running his hands through his wiry hair while he reads the Sunday newspaper*

Step 4: Describe the hands themselves, in detail. What do they look like? How do they feel?

Example: *too pale, with blue veins standing up*
cool and dry

Step 5: Create a simile or metaphor. What do the person's hands resemble? What do they remind you of?

Example: *The hands are like gnarly tree roots.*

Step 6: Write down the two questions you asked the person earlier as a homework assignment. Choose the question that seems to fit best into the scene you have been setting in Steps 1 - 5.

Example: *Why do you read so much?*

Step 7: Write down the answer you recorded earlier to the question in Step 6.

Example: *Because I have to. It's like breathing, to me.*

Now you are ready to go on to the next stages of writing your poem. See "Extracting a Poem," "Revising" and "Sharing" (pages 135-153).

My mother is sleeping
in the afternoon air,
breathing slowly,
in her comfortable bed.
Her hands lie
on a soft pillow made of cotton.
They are textured roughly,
but soft, and smell of dough,
like a baker's hands.
Her hands are cool and fresh
as the morning air.
I ask her slowly,
"How do you survive this?
Sleeping in the day,
working at night,
taking care of two kids
and yourself
at the same time?"
She replies,
"I barely do,"
and puts her head down
and goes to sleep again.

— Travis M. Holt, 4th grade

My father works
in wet cement all day.
Even wearing gloves,
his hands are as rough
as sandpaper, as rough
as a pine cone.
"Why are your hands so rough?
Why are your hands so hot?"
"Because I am a hot-blooded man
in a cold hard job."

— Jamie L. Osborne, 4th grade

My grandma patiently
working out our family's
kinks and troubles
makes pie in between times
Pulling, rolling,
patting the dough
with flour
Kneading, massaging
out the lumps
with freckled hands
as soft and supple as her dough
Why knead the bread
so long?
So our pie doesn't fall apart.

— Amy Rider, college

Student Memory

With "Student Memory," students explore their feelings about being a student and about school. Before students begin writing, spend some time helping them to recall vivid school memories. Ask them about kindergarten and first grade. What do they remember most? What about later years? Suggest that they think about awards, embarrassing moments, sports events, arguments, incidents that made them laugh, etc.

Suggested Readings

Norton Anthology of Modern Poetry

"The Life Ahead," Philip Levine, page 1296

"Oranges," Gary Soto, page 1689

"Indian Boarding School: The Runaways," Louise Erdrich, page 1720

Student Memory

Nearly everyone has strong memories — both good and bad — about school. Write a poem about one of those memories, and, at the same time, make it clear how you feel about school in general.

It may help you to sit back and think for a few minutes about school as a whole. What do you like about going to school? What do you dislike? What has school given you? What has it taken away from you?

In choosing a memory to write about, try to pick one that is clear and strong. As you complete the word gathering steps below, write whatever comes to mind. You can sift it out later, when you actually start composing your poem.

Word Gathering

Step 1: How do you feel about being in school? List words that specifically express your attitude toward school and your role as a student.

Examples: *I love school.*
I like friends, involvement, meeting people.

Step 2: Think of one strong memory about school, from previous years. Describe the memory in present tense (as though it is happening right now). Focus on details.

Examples: *I am in first grade, and it is the first day of school.*
A boy named Charlie keeps staring and staring at me.
I wonder what's wrong with me.

Step 3: Describe how you felt on the day of the memory. Use all your senses. What did you see? Feel? Hear? Smell? Taste? Again, write in present tense.

Examples: *I see the big yellow bus coming down the road.*
I touch the soft plaid of my new shirt.
I hear the big kids from fourth grade coming down the street, laughing, and I feel left out and different.

Step 4: How long has it been since that strongest student memory? How have you changed?

Examples: *That was eight years ago.*
Now I belong. Now I laugh with the big kids.

Step 5: Make a list of things you are asked to do as a student. The tone of this list should reflect your attitude toward school. For example, if you think school is boring, you should list things you do in school that you find boring. If you think school is a lot of fun, you should list things that you enjoy.

Examples: *learn my part for the play*
try out for first chair clarinet

Step 6: Create a simile or metaphor comparing yourself to something associated with school.

Example: *I feel as popular as the Coke machine during afternoon break.*

Now you are ready to go on to the next stages of writing your poem. See "Extracting a Poem," "Revising" and "Sharing" (pages 135-153).

SCHOOL

School is disgusting,
it causes disturbing thoughts.
I'd rather be the cafeteria food
that just sits there and rots.
School bites,
it's really boring.
I have better things to do
than sit there snoring.

One day, I was in a fight
with a kid who's insane.
We tumbled over the desks,
but I could feel no pain.
We fought and tumbled onto the floor
and when the fight was over,
I was sent out the door.

School is so hard,
the days are so long.
The teachers are always on my case,
saying everything I do is wrong.

I hang out with Steven,
he's my best friend.
We'll always be buddies,
hopefully to the end.

I go to sleep when I feel like it
and that's pretty late;
my life is really busy,
I thrive at a high rate.

School's pretty boring;
I wish it would take a new route.
It makes me feel like an old book
which is never checked out.

— Randall M. Reynolds, 7th grade

ANN

arbitrary categories
senseless separations
girls/boys
math/English
p.e./music
(where does art go?)
fractions, subtractions
divisions and
(God forbid)
radicals
it started in kindergarten
with floppy dolls
on bathroom doors
Raggedy Ann for girls
Andy for the boys
But I'm wearing pants.
Better go with Andy.
Before I get in
Mrs. Smith dashes over
knocks me down
then sweeps me up
sends me back to Ann
Immediately I suspect
conspiracy
What was Andy hiding?

— Amy Rider, college

ANGER

The "Anger" exercise helps students explore and express feelings about the emotion of anger, through poetry.

Prepare students for writing by asking them to remember times in their life when they felt extremely angry. Explain that they don't need to recount the incidents in the poem; they just need to remember them as they write.

Anger

When you write a poem about anger, you need to really *think* about anger. What makes you mad? How do you feel when you are mad? How do you deal with your anger? It helps to remember specific incidents that have made you mad in the past.

Follow the word gathering steps below to help you collect words, phrases and sentences about anger. Don't agonize over the questions. Just write down what comes to mind. Let the ideas flow. Later you will choose the best words and start composing a poem. Remember that anger is a strong emotion. Use strong words to describe it.

Word Gathering

Step 1: What colors do you see when you are angry? What color is your brain when you get mad?

Examples: *deep violet streaks*
My brain turns icy white.

Step 2: Make a list of things that make you angry. Be as specific as possible.

Example: *being treated like a dumb kid*
having to pay for a glass of water
getting blamed for something I didn't do

Step 3: How do you act when you get mad? Do you cry, turn red, yell, hit something, or what? What happens to your body when you feel anger? Be specific.

Example: *I try not to cry but usually do.*
I freeze up and won't talk.
My jaw clenches.
My eyes swell and turn red.

Step 4: Describe how you get out of an angry mood.

Example: *I usually go to my room, get under my down comforter and watch corny old tv shows on Nickelodeon.*

Step 5: Describe how you feel once your anger has subsided. What colors do you see when you are no longer angry? What color is your brain when you are no longer mad? How do you feel?

Example: *Everything turns to lilac as I mellow out into sleep.*
My brain turns a soft shade of rose.
I feel exhausted.

Now you are ready to go on to the next stages of writing your poem. See "Extracting a Poem," "Revising" and "Sharing" (pages 135-153).

ANGER

The colors are red streaking through
like a red racer,
black curving in with blotches
of a desolate gray.
Big black spiders creep across my ceiling.
I gasp for air,
an explosion of wetness falls from my eyes.
I take gasps.
I release my anger from within
by saying out loud my feelings.
Soon, it is gone.
I fall asleep.
In my dreams, I feel guilt.
I feel relief from all problems.
I see a glowing lavender.

— Shelby Walker, 6th grade

ANGER

Anger strikes
All I see becomes dark blue,
My brain turns blood red.
Anger strikes.
I try to speak,
Nobody listens!
I don't get the respect I deserve.
Anger strikes.
My jaws clench.
I want to hit
Scream in frustration.
Anger strikes.
Time alone will cool me off.
I'm tired, depressed.
Everything becomes a softer shade.
Anger has struck.

— Zac Curtis, high school

Bright orange like supernovas
fiery red when worlds burn
my brain pumps out streams of adrenaline

telephone ringing annoys me
insults to my intelligence annoy me
I complain about my cats and the smell
of crab
My grandma's handwriting confuses me
I get intensely angry when people
embarrass me

I wait to cool down and seek deep
isolation
when I am calm I see deep blue like
ocean bottoms
My brain sends out endorphins.

— Jon Phillip Davis, Jr., 6th grade

A Verb and a Verb

With "A Verb and a Verb," students explore the relationship between two verbs.

The assignment provides an excellent opportunity for helping students learn more about parts of speech. It also gives them practice in using the dictionary and looking closely at the meanings of words.

Students will need dictionaries for this exercise.

Suggested Readings

Piping Down the Valleys Wild

"Tiptoe," Karla Kuskin, page 3

"Full of the Moon," Karla Kuskin, page 53

A VERB AND A VERB

"A Verb and a Verb" gives you a chance to write an action poem. Choose a verb that has something to do with you and your experiences. If you are a gymnast, you might pick a verb like *balance* or *tumble.* If you love to eat potato chips, you might choose the verb *crunch.* If you like to write notes to your friends, you might choose a verb like *scribble* or *gossip.*

After you have selected a verb, complete the word gathering steps below. As you write, try not to think about your final poem. Just concentrate on choosing interesting words. Later you will sift through what you have written and make choices about what to include in a poem. Remember, you won't include everything.

WORD GATHERING

Step 1: Write down the verb you have chosen. This verb will be the title of your poem.

Example: *laugh*

Step 2: Using the dictionary, write down all the definitions of your verb.

Examples: *to show mirth, joy or scorn with a smile or chuckle and explosive sound; to find amusement or pleasure in something*

Step 3: Create several sentences that use the verb. Make the sentences describe your own personal experiences.

Examples: *I laughed when I saw my brother slip in the orange juice he had spilled.*
I laughed when my friend Astrid pretended to be a rap star.

Step 4: Mark the sentence you like best from Step 3. Now write several sentences about the same subject, but using different forms of the verb.

Examples: *I* ***was laughing*** *hysterically at my brother when I saw him fall.*

I ***will laugh*** *at him if I want to.*
He ***will be laughing*** *about it later.*
I ***laugh*** *at my brother a lot.*
I ***laughed*** *out loud when I saw him sprawl on the floor.*

Step 5: Choose the three sentences you like best from Step 4.

Step 6: Choose a second verb. This verb should have a meaningful relationship to the first verb. For example, it might have an opposite meaning. (*laughed/cried*). It might have a similar meaning (*laugh/giggle*). It might show a result. (For example, if you *laugh* a lot, the result might be that you *glow.*)

Example: *laugh/cry*

Step 7: Write several sentences using both your first and second verb (or different forms of the verbs). Make these sentences about the same experience that you wrote about in Steps 4 and 5.

Examples: *I laughed so hard I started crying.*
Why do laughing and crying both make tears run down my cheeks?

(Optional)
Step 8: Using the dictionary, write down the definitions of your second verb.

Examples: *weep, sob, wail*

Now you are ready to go on to the next stages of writing your poem. See "Extracting a Poem," "Revising" and "Sharing" (pages 135-153).

CLIMB

Climb: to go up
or down
by use of the hands
and feet
I used to climb
the cabinets in our kitchen
Door handles and
drawer handles became
grips
as I clambered
up the cupboards
full of china.
I was climbing
for crackers
and Cheerios
and puffed up marshmallows.
I've scaled mountains, too,
but the snowy reward
was never so great
as the marshmallow
creme in our cabinet.

— Amy Rider, college

SNUB

Snub means
to treat coldly
to be scornful
to act with contempt.

You can snub your neighbors
by ignoring them.
I am going to snub you.
I snubbed him last week.
Have you ever snubbed someone?

Snubbing your friends
is not very nice,
thoughtful, kind, refined or mannered.

— Lindsay Jones, 6th grade

The Blazon

With this exercise, students practice writing a specific form — the blazon. The blazon is a list poem that compares the writer's physical and personal characteristics with nature. A blazon can be a complete poem in itself, or it can be a poetry form used within another type of poem.

Project Ideas

Students may enjoy drawing or painting the comparisons they make in their poems. The artistic renderings can make an excellent display for parents' night or other public events.

Suggested Readings

The blazon is a very popular form in contemporary Native American verse. A good anthology to refer to is *Songs from the Earth on Turtle's Back*, edited by Joseph Bruchac (Greenfield Review Press, Greenfield Center, New York, 1983).

The Blazon

When you write a blazon, you compare your physical and personal characteristics with things found in nature. You *list* the comparisons, just as you would list items in a grocery list. Nature is full of things that lend themselves to comparison — oceans, air, trees, animals, bird songs, plants, minerals, land forms and more.

Begin your blazon by following the word gathering steps below. Don't censor yourself, and try not to analyze too much. Your comparisons may sometimes be a stretch, but that's okay. You will have a chance later to pick and choose what you want to keep and what you want to throw away.

Try to make your comparisons original. People are always comparing eyes to stars, for example, in statements like this: "Her eyes are like stars; they twinkle in the night." Instead of comparing your eyes to stars, compare them to something else, like dark clay around a stream or the metallic shine of a gold fish swimming in the sunlight. If you take a little time, you will be able to come up with new ways of saying things.

Word Gathering

Step 1: List the personal characteristics that you want to write about in your blazon. The list should be fairly extensive and should include both physical characteristics and characteristics you can't see.

Examples: *my hair, my eyes, my laugh*
thoughts, spirit, energy

Step 2: Compare each item on your list to something in nature.

Example: *My hair is tangled and wild, like a tumbleweed.*

Step 3: Compare your poem itself to something in nature. Complete the phrase, "My poem is . . ." by creating as many metaphors as you can. These metaphors can be single words or complex phrases.

Examples: *My poem is a wheat field blowing in a breeze.*
My poem is a crow calling out.

Step 4: Complete the phrase, "I am . . ." with as many metaphors as you can from nature. Again, these metaphors can be single words or complex phrases.

Examples: *I am the wind.*
I am a cactus hiding inside my prickly exterior.

(Optional)
Step 5: Complete the poem by creating one last metaphor — a "you" and "I" comparison. You decide who "you" is.

Example: *You are the sun, and I am a plant soaking up your warm rays.*

Now you are ready to go on to the next stages of writing your poem. See "Extracting a Poem," "Revising" and "Sharing" (pages 135-153).

I AM

My mind is a river
widening into a vast ocean.
My arms are the branches of a tree
swaying in a gale.
My chest is the trunk of a tree,
stirring only slightly
in the harsh wind and rain.
My legs are roots
gripping the cold, moist earth.
My poem is an immense forest of possibilities
stretching endlessly
to the four corners of the world.
I am but a small sapling,
deep in the heart of the forest.
You are the window and I am the air
passing through you as easily
as fish glide through the water.

— Gabe Nelson, 6th grade

BOASTING

My hands are eagle claws.
My fingers are worms in the dirt.
My eyes look into the future.
My feet are wild horse's hooves
running along the land.
My shoulders are the flat rocks
near the rivers.
My shadow brings the night.
My spirit makes the world go round.
My bones hold the world together.
My poem is the light of the world.
I am the sun that reflects
off of snow and water.
You are the grass in the meadow
and I am the sun
that will dry you out.

— Jacob Meng, 6th grade

My jeans, laced with holes, are like a tree:
home to a woodpecker.
My old worn flannel is like so many rocks:
smoothed by the ocean.
My hair is like brushed seaweed:
not blonde, but still catching the sun.
My skin is a shaved peach.

My eyes are like cratered redwood bark.
My poem is like a brick,
it is like a coral reef,

it is like a feather.
I am like a crow. I am like a magpie.

I am like the raven that sits and waits for you.
You are the sleeping man in the field
and I am the raven who pecks your eyes
in your slumber.

— Erin Sullivan Meyer, 8th grade

FREE SPIRIT

My spirit, a bird that flies high.
My fingers, slick as ten snakes.
My hands, rough as rigid stones.
My arms, the power of two grizzlies.
My hair, wavy ripples on a pond's surface.
My poem is the wood in the forest
and the leaves on the trees.
I am the woods and the water.
I am the world and the universe.
You are the animal that hibernates.
I am the cave that provides shelter.
I am everything.

— Daniel Reynolds, 6th grade

Autobiographical Poem

With "Autobiographical Poem," students take a look at themselves through comparing themselves to an animal. They also work on using consistent images in a poem, to create unity.

Notes

In helping students understand consistent images, you might use an example from sports. A sportscaster wouldn't want to say something like this:

Joe Schmoe is as fast as a jaguar as he runs up and down the court. He is as aggressive as a freight train. He is also as graceful as a ballet dancer.

All those images are confusing. It's hard to picture Joe. It would be much more effective to stick to the jaguar image, perhaps like this:

Joe Schmoe is as fast and as aggressive as a jaguar as he runs up and down the court. He also shows the jaguar's grace as he shoots the ball and scores.

Suggested Readings

Norton Anthology of Modern Poetry

"Fern Hill," Dylan Thomas, page 925

"The Tourist from Syracuse," Donald Justice, page 1152

"So I Said I Am Ezra," A.R. Ammons, page 1167

"Wodwo," Ted Hughes, page 1401

"This Is a Photograph of Me," Margaret Atwood, page 1543

"Daguerreotype Taken in Old Age," Margaret Atwood, page 1545

AUTOBIOGRAPHICAL POEM

What subject do you probably know best in the world? Yourself. That's why *you* make a perfect subject for a poem.

As you complete the word gathering steps below, try to be consistent in the images you create. In other words, don't jump around, creating a metaphor about butterflies, then about giraffes, then about groundhogs. If you compare yourself first to a butterfly, for example, try to create images that involve colors and wind and trees — all things that are appropriate to butterflies. Skip creating a simile about your hair and a goldfish, even though such a simile might be just perfect for a different poem.

WORD GATHERING

Step 1: Describe your physical appearance. Focus on interesting details that you like about yourself, or that you think others like about you. Think about the unique features that make you who you are.

Example: *I have a smile that makes others want to smile, too.*
spirals of curly hair springing up all over my head

Step 2: Compare yourself to an animal. If you were an animal, what species would you be? What animal has similar features?

Example: *I'd be a puppy because puppies make people want to smile, too.*

Step 3: What color (or colors) is the animal you would be? Create a simile or metaphor that compares the color to something in nature.

Example: *Golden retriever puppy — a golden rust color, like leaves in the fall*

Step 4: Describe the mannerisms and poses that distinguish you.

Example: *I wave my hands a lot when I talk.*
I sometimes get excited and talk with my mouth full.
I laugh a lot.

Step 5: Describe characteristics and personality traits that you most like about yourself.

Examples: *I have a good sense of humor.*
People can trust me.
I'm kind.

Step 6: Describe what positive actions you could do with the characteristics you described in Step 5.

Examples: *I can make people laugh.*
People can talk to me about their problems because I won't blab to the world.

Step 7: List some of your fears and their opposites.

Examples: *getting a terrible disease — staying healthy*
guns — peace
I'm afraid of disappointing my dad — making him proud
Sometimes I'm afraid of the dark — light

Step 8: Create a metaphor by comparing the pairs of opposites to nature. Make your metaphor fit the imagery you have been developing. For example, if most of your imagery has been about trees, don't suddenly jump to a metaphor about an African elephant.

Examples: *A tree is disappointed when it droops with an early, heavy snow, and it is proud when it reaches out to the sun with new buds.*
Darkness and light are the bark on an aspen tree at dusk.

Now you are ready to go on to the next stages of writing your poem. See "Extracting a Poem," "Revising" and "Sharing" (pages 135-153).

wild, laughing green eyes
in a pale setting
a perky cat, ready to pounce
crazy, as a flash of lightning
listening, talking
lively, loud, courageous
I can brighten someone's day.
loneliness
friendship
a lost kitten
finds its mother

— Karis C. Triska, 6th grade

tall
hazel, twinkling eyes
a lily
as blue as ocean water

at ease in a sunlit room
thinking
of strolling along the current
at the beach

war
peace
tumbling waves
calm water

— Rebecca Lindsay, 6th grade

THE ANT — AN AUTOBIOGRAPHY

Hoop earring
an ornament
like antennae
can be intimidating.
Brown outer layer
same color
as the muck through which
we dig.
Don't go
too deep
for being buried
alive
is as bad as being
fried.

— Christopher Markuson, college

Deep brown eyes
that have not yet been explored
a dolphin making
blue ripples in the cool ocean water
I frolic under the moonlight sky
a crab, can he survive
the cold, harsh ocean world?

— Tibi Girczyc-Blum, 6th grade

Dark, almost black hair,
like the plumage of a giant eagle
that soars high, alive and free . . .

A brook, clear blue,
runs smoothly between its banks by day,
while by night, it rushes swift and dark,
like Death . . .

A boy in the ancient forest,
observing the slightest movements,
sounds, scents;
he fears the owl,
the owl that hunts,
that hunts like a shadow.

— Duncan Ralph, 6th grade

MODEL POEM

This exercise uses a published poem as a model to help students learn to generate their own questions for the word gathering step of the poem-writing process. "Model Poem" is intended as a transition, helping students move from the exercises (and their provided prompts) to the freedom of writing on their own.

MODEL POEM

You are almost ready to write a poem entirely on your own. First, however, you need to learn how to create your own questions for word gathering.

First read the poem below:

THE BEAUTY OF MOUNTAIN AND WATER: FISHING

(1) Yesterday I was going to fish the Eel River
but it rained,
(2) and it rained today, but now
the evening sun swims on the horizon.
(3) Water shines on river rock.
A few drops of mist spatter
herons and gulls toward night roosts.
Fat cows feed along the banks.
(4) I wait for the wind to clear the fog
so I can enjoy the rising moon
through the redwoods.

(5) As the fog rolls back out of the valley,
one by one, the poles of fishermen appear
stretching into the far bend.
(6) Hooks question the water,
the fish answer,
knives interrupt and interpret.

(7) I stop, wait, rest;
the river walks off by itself.
The clouds swim with the current.
In the full water, the dry leaves of willows
lift sails to the breeze.
(8) I think of the fist
swimming in the pools
crowded with azalea petals,
and I know that I am alive.
My life is full. I am calm
(9) The sun shines a rainbow
above the riffle;
(10) I release a wild steelhead.

— Benjamin Green

Notice that the poem has been broken into numbered sections. For each section, write a question that might have prompted the poet to answer with those lines of poetry. In other words, imagine that the lines of poetry are the poet's response to your word gathering prompt.

Your questions should not be specific to the poem. They should be more general in nature. For example, don't ask, "Why didn't you go fishing?" Instead say, "What happened to prevent you from taking part in an activity you enjoy?"

After you have written questions for each numbered section of "The Beauty of Mountain and Water: Fishing," put the poem away. Then answer the questions yourself, based on your own experiences. Treat the questions you have written as if they were word gathering prompts like the ones in the exercises you have already completed.

Model Poem

QUESTIONS AND RESPONSES:

Step 1: What event happened that postponed the activity you enjoy?

Our football team was going to play the final game of the season. But the pouring rain never let up so it was postponed.

Step 2: How does the incident that postponed your activity affect your surroundings?

The grass is wet and everything looks bleak and everybody who came leaves disappointed.

Step 3: Explain in detail what the surroundings look like.

There are dark clouds in the sky and the rain falls down so hard it stings my face.

Step 4: When do you resume your activity?

The next day I get up excitedly anxious for the game that was delayed.

Step 5: What does the place where you perform your activity look like?

The stands sit there like giant walls closing me in forcing me to move forward.

Step 6: How do you perform your activity?

I am ready. I hear every breath and heartbeat. Quarterback screams hike then shoves the ball into my chest as I bolt forward passing men as big as freight trains. I move in a poetic motion as I rocket past them like a missile. Huge giants crash behind like thunder missing me by smallest margins.

Step 7: Look around at the surroundings. What do you see?

The fans on their feet. Other team shattered.

Step 8: How do you feel at that moment?

Invincible as I stand there.

Step 9: Look at the scenery. What does it look like?

Surroundings are the same but I belong here.

Step 10: How do you finish off the activity?

We have emerged victorious.

RESULTING POEM:

We were going to play.
The pouring rain
never lets up.
Postponement.
Everything
looks bleak.
The rain falls down so hard
it stings my face.
The next day
I walk
onto the field.
The stands sit there
like giant walls
closing
me in.
I am ready.
I can hear every breath
and heartbeat.
The ball
is shoved
into my chest.
I bolt forward
passing men
as big
as towering redwoods
I move
in a poetic motion
as I rocket past
them like an atomic bomb
ready to detonate.
Huge giants
crash
behind me
like a wrecking ball
demolishing an old
brick building.
The fans are on
their feet.
The other team shattered.
I belong here.

— Zachary Howard, 9th grade

DESIGN A POEM

This exercise helps students learn to write poems about subjects of their own choosing, without the prompts from an established exercise.

DESIGN A POEM

By following the steps in different exercises from *Beyond Roses Are Red, Violets Are Blue,* you have been writing poems while learning the *process* of poetry writing.

Now that you know about word gathering, writing, polishing and revising, you are ready to design your own poem-writing exercises. Follow the steps below to create your own poem.

Step 1: Choose a topic with a narrow focus. In other words, be specific.

Step 2: Create a list of questions or steps to follow for word gathering. Follow these guidelines:

A. Include at least one question that tells what or who the subject *is.*

B. Include at least one question that helps create an objective description of the topic. In other words, ask a question that generates the facts, without opinion.

C. Include at least one question that is subjective. In other words, ask a question that includes personal opinions.

D. Ask for at least one simile or metaphor.

E. Limit yourself to eight questions/steps at this time. Try to make up your own questions, but feel free to borrow or adapt from the list below.

- Describe your subject.
- What do you see, hear, taste, feel, smell?
- Create a metaphor or simile involving your subject.
- If your subject could talk, what would it say?
- What is happening (or happened)? Tell just the facts.
- How do you feel about what is happening (or happened)?

Step 3: Complete your "Word Gathering" by answering the questions and/or following the steps you have chosen.

Step 4: Now you are ready to go on to the next stages of writing your poem. See "Extracting a Poem," "Revising" and "Sharing" (pages 135-153).

QUESTIONS AND RESPONSES:

Step 1: Think about a moment when you grew up a little bit.

When I got my ears pierced.

Step 2: Describe yourself before this experience happened.

small brown boyish with Dorothy Hamill hairdo your basic tomboy with scabby knees and mosquito bite scars

Step 3: Describe the experience itself. What happened? What is the setting? When did it happen? Who was there? Think about the sounds, sights, smells.

5th birthday. Mom and Grandma marched me through the big mall doors holding my tiny hands at the shop they lifted me into the big blue swively chair. bright lights. antiseptic. big blue gun the woman used to shoot my ear with an earring.

Step 4: How did you feel? Use a metaphor to describe your reaction to the experience.

small sharp pain, but I didn't cry. held back the tears like a cloudy day that doesn't rain.

Step 5: Describe how the experience changed you physically and mentally? How did you grow up a little bit?

tiny blue sparkles dotted my ears. brave and strong. one step closer to being a woman

RESULTING POEM:

GETTING MY EARS PIERCED

Small brown and boyish
with a Dorothy Hamill hairdo.
Your basic tomboy with
scabby knees and mosquito bite scars.

My fifth birthday.

Mom and Grandma marched me through
the big mall doors
each holding one tiny hand.
At the shop they lifted me into the
big blue swively chair.
Bright lights. Antiseptic. And a . . .
Big Blue Gun.
Shot through the ear.
Small sharp pain,
but I didn't cry.
Held back the tears like a
cloudy day that doesn't rain.

Brave and strong
with tiny blue sparkles dotting my ears.
One step closer to being a woman.

— Marie DiPrince, college student

Extracting a Poem

Extracting a Poem

When students have completed the word gathering steps for an exercise, they are ready to begin the next step: extracting a poem. For examples of actual student work in completing this step, see the Appendix, "The Middleground Method in Action," pages 157-161.

Extracting a Poem
A Review

Extracting a poem is a three-part process:

Choosing the best words. First students should go through their word gathering material and circle the "best" words from each step. The best words will be the ones that:

- give the most important and accurate information
- use the most interesting and original language
- create the most vivid pictures in the reader's mind
- "sound" the best

Using the best words to create the rough draft of a poem. After they have circled the best words and phrases, have students start creating lines for their poem, using the words they have circled. Ask them to create only one or two lines from each step, in the order the steps are given. (Assure students that they will be able to reword and rearrange their lines later, if they find it necessary.)

Because writing poetry is new to students, most will want to write full sentences that stretch from margin to margin. To keep them focused on writing verse, have them fold their writing paper in thirds. The narrow writing space helps them keep their lines short. You might also mention that lines of a poem are rarely more than eight or nine words long.

It is also important to talk about the reasons for line breaks. Poets usually use a line break for these reasons:

- to let the reader take a breath
- to indicate that the reader should pause
- to slow down the poem with short lines or speed it up with long lines
- to form a certain pattern on the page, or to stress certain words by putting them at the beginning or at the end of a line.

Encourage students to keep their poems short, tight and concentrated. Dynamism and tension are created when poems are kept short. By choosing only one or two lines to include, per prompt, students are learning to discriminate between their best writing and their weaker writing. You might return to the clothes closet analogy: even with a full closet, a person still has to choose the best outfit; he or she can't wear three pairs of pants and six shirts at one time. Narrowing down the choices will result in a much better outfit.

Playing with the rough draft and creating a not-so-rough draft. Before students are finished with the extracting step, they need to play with their lines until the poem reads smoothly and makes sense. In other words, they need to take their rough draft and turn it into a not-so-rough draft. Students, before they complete the extracting step, should have a not-so-rough draft that they are willing to share and take to the next step, revising.

REVISING

REVISING

When students have completed a not-so-rough draft of a poem, they are ready to begin revising the poem. For examples of actual student work in completing this step, see the Appendix, "The Middleground Method in Action," pages 157-161.

Revising
A Review

Revising is a necessary and important part of the writing process. Revising means literally "to see again" and to see through the reader's eyes. Too often students think what they have written is good, not because it *is* good but because they have written it. Students must realize that their not-so-rough drafts are only a beginning that can be made better.

While word gathering allows students to be spontaneous and personal, revising is more impersonal. It switches the focus from the writer's experience to the words that describe that experience.

The first part of the revision process is to have students use questions from the "Revision Checklist" (page 143) to take a look at how their poems are crafted. Using the questions from the checklist to guide them, students should first revise their work without feedback.

Next they can get feedback from others. Before the high school level, that feedback will likely be from you, the teacher. (Response groups are not usually useful with younger students because they are not yet at a developmental level where they are able to judge the quality of another's work, or even their own work. If response groups are used, it should be as a supplement to teacher feedback.)

Teachers often avoid commenting on students' creative work, worrying that their response will be merely subjective. However, the response to a poem *must* be subjective. After all, poems are written to elicit an emotional response and to receive any reader's opinion can be valuable to the poet. As a teacher responding to a student's poem, you also can use the questions from the "Revision Checklist" as a guideline.

Another idea is to have some students volunteer to write their drafts on the board to be used as a group revision exercise. Using the "Revision Checklist," the teacher and the class together can suggest tentative changes to the sample poems, leaving the final decisions about whether or not to take those suggestions, of course, to the author. This process can help all the students better understand how to approach the revision of their own poems. They will get ideas for their own work.

Revision is the chance to change one's mind. After completing the "Revision Checklist" and listening to the feedback of others, a student may want to make adjustments. He or she may want to add new ideas and/or new details, or to delete words and images that do not contribute to the poem's momentum.

A student may even discover that what is written does not, after all, express his or her ideas and feelings. If so, the student may choose to try the steps in "A Second Way to Look at Revision" (page 145). The techniques in this list provide very effective techniques for approaching the poem in a totally different way.

The revision process should continue until the work is finished. You should allow plenty of time for the process because real revision does take time. In fact, it's a good idea to let some work "sit" for extended periods, coming back to the revision process more than once throughout the school year. Students are often able to be more objective about their work after some time has elapsed and it seems less personal to them.

REVISION CHECKLIST

Have you ever said something you regretted and wished you could take it back? If so, you were wishing for revision — the ability to go back and say just the right thing in just the right way.

Revising is one of the most important steps in writing a poem. Don't be surprised if your poem takes many forms before you are finished with it. Use the following questions to help you with the revision process:

COMMON SENSE CHECK

- Does your poem say what you want it to say? Is the message clear?
- Does your poem make sense all the way through? Are the lines in the best order? Have you kept the same point of view? (For example, if you start out describing a flower through the eyes of an elderly gentleman, you probably don't want to have one line describing the flower from your own point of view.)
- Are you happy with the poem?
- Think of your poem as a picture, full of images. Are all the images appropriate to the feeling you want to convey? (For example, if your poem is about the peace you feel on summer mornings, you probably don't want a bloody-mouthed polar bear roaring through the scene.)
- Have you kept the same tense throughout the poem? (For example, if you start out saying "I *see*" and "I *want*," you probably don't want to switch to "I *saw*" and "I *wanted*" later in the poem.)

TOO MUCH/TOO LITTLE CHECK

- Are there parts of the poem that need to be expanded with more detail or more explanation?
- Are there enough details to make readers see what you want them to see?
- Are there parts of the poem that are unnecessary or irrelevant and that could be deleted?

BEGINNING/ENDING CHECK

- Look at your poem's opening lines. Do they capture a reader's interest?
- Look at your poem's concluding lines. Does the ending provide a sense of closure? Is the last line a memorable one?

Sound Check

- Read your poem aloud. How does it sound? Are there any words, lines or phrases that stick out and ruin the rhythm or feeling of your poem?
- Again, read your poem aloud. Have you emphasized the most interesting or important words by placing them at the beginning or the end of your lines?

Wilted Lettuce Check

- When you create a salad, the last thing you want is a dish full of nothing but boring, wilted lettuce. When you create a poem, the last thing you want is lines full of boring, wilted-lettuce kinds of words. Are the words you have chosen fresh and crisp and interesting?
- Is every word necessary? Does every word add something to the poem?

The Quiet as a Mouse Check

- Even the best poets can fall into the trap of using clichés like "He was as quiet as a mouse" or "Her eyes twinkled like stars." Do you see any clichés you could eliminate or replace?

The Shape Check

- How does your poem look on the page? Does it have an interesting and appealing shape?
- Are the lines of a sensible length?
- Look at the line breaks. Do your line breaks make sense?
- Look at your stanza breaks. A stanza in a poem is the equivalent of a paragraph in prose. Poets usually use stanzas to group related thoughts, to show a certain order of ideas or to indicate a long pause with white space. Do you have a reason for your stanza breaks?

The Polishing Check

- Are all your words spelled correctly?
- Is the writing legible and neat?
- If you are writing in grammatically correct form, is the grammar correct?
- If you are punctuating the poem, is the punctuation correct?

A Second Way to Look at Revision

If you aren't pleased with an early draft of your poem, try any of the following techniques. They can help you start over or see your poem in a new way.

1. Rewrite the poem from memory. Chances are that you will remember only the strongest and freshest language and the most memorable experiences. Use what you remember, and build on that.
2. Read the poem as if it were a conversation. If you were listening to this conversation, what questions would you ask? The answers to those questions are probably details that the poem must have to make it clear and interesting to a reader.
3. Change the way the poem looks. Change the indentation. Create a shape. Break the poem into shorter or longer lines, shorter or longer stanzas. See if the new shape reveals any new meaning.
4. Write two stanzas beyond the current ending. Maybe your poem is not yet finished.
5. Delete two stanzas of your poem. Maybe your poem states more than is needed.
6. Circle the most interesting words in the poem. Write more about these words. Substitute some of the new writing for the uncircled parts.
7. Circle the most interesting words. See if the poem makes sense using only the circled words. Delete everything that is unnecessary.
8. Write the poem as one long sentence, and see what results.
9. Double-space the poem. Then add new lines between each of the original lines.
10. "Slice" the poem into single lines. Then reassemble the lines into the best reading order.
11. At random, delete every fourth (or some other arbitrarily chosen number) word. Then try to come up with new words that fit.

SHARING

SHARING

After a student has completed a poem, the next step is sharing. There are many ways for students to share a poem with others.

Sharing
A Review

Sharing can take many forms, including classroom and public readings and publishing in newspapers, magazines, books, classroom anthologies or personal collections. Students can also share by exhibiting their work in school and public displays or by creating posters and other forms of artwork that incorporate poetry.

Readings. One method of sharing poetry is through readings. Students enjoy performance. However, like poetry writing, performance requires practice. Students should read their poems aloud several times before reciting to an audience. It is helpful for them to listen to recordings of other poets reading, to hear how professionals deliver their work.

Students should also follow these reading aloud basics:

- Stand and face the audience.
- Wait until you have the audience's attention.
- Announce the poem, giving its title and any explanation you would like to share.
- Pause and count to three.
- Read aloud in a loud, slow, deliberate but natural voice. (Be sure the reading copy is neat and legible.)

It may take several attempts for students to enunciate all words clearly, but with each practice, their performance will improve.

Every reading includes two parts: the reader and the listener. Each has a role. For classroom readings, student audiences usually need instruction on their role. The student audience needs to be attentive, not making faces, giggling or laughing. There should be no eye rolling, yawns of boredom or nose picking. Neighbors should not goose neighbors. Applause is appropriate at the end of each reading. These simple and humorous warnings are usually enough. Even in classrooms where the writing sessions have been a bit chaotic, students are typically respectful of their peers during performances.

A classroom reading is a positive beginning, a time for practice and sharing, but an open reading in front of parents, family or the whole school is a major event for students. A public reading at a local coffee house for those students who have truly written accomplished poems is a legitimate reward.

Publishing. Seeing their work in print is another form of recognition for student poets and another way for them to share their work.

Classroom anthologies are one effective way to share student poems. Students choose their best work for publication, and they can often act as their own editors, typists and assemblers. (For younger students, teacher and parent volunteers can do the work.) Many schools have binding machines, and local photocopy centers or printers can also bind the books in a variety of inexpensive ways.

Having students submit poems for publication can also be an excellent learning experience and a reward for achievement. See "How to Prepare a Manuscript," page 151, and "Periodicals that Accept Children/Teen/Young Adult Work," page 152.

Exhibits. Another way to share poems is through school exhibits or public displays. Students can display the poems alone or as part of posters and other forms of artwork. Many of the exercises in this book suggest specific projects for different poems.

How to Prepare a Manuscript

When you submit a poem for publication, you should be familiar with the marketplace. That means you should know as much as possible about a publication before you send in your work for consideration.

How do you find out about publications you haven't read? First write and request sample copies and/or writers' guidelines. The writers' guidelines will tell you important information about the magazine, like what kinds of material it publishes, helpful hints for first-time authors and material the editors are *not* interested in receiving. Always include a self-addressed stamped envelope (SASE) with your letter. Poetry publishers operate on a very tight budget, and they often can't send out materials unless postage is provided.

When you receive sample copies and guidelines, see which ones are best suited for the kind of poems you have written.

For most publications, writers should submit three to five poems. They should be typed on good quality white paper. The poems should be single-spaced, with one-inch margins on all sides of the paper. Your name, address and age should be included in an upper corner. The title should be typed in all capital letters, and there should be two lines between the title and the first line of the poem. Type only one poem to a page. Make sure each poem submitted is error-free. Fold the entire submission in thirds, not each individual poem.

Next comes the cover letter. Most editors appreciate a personal letter that tells them who you are and why you are submitting work to them. Here's how to format a cover letter:

- Type your name and address in the upper left corner.
- Skip a line and type the date of submission.
- Skip a line and type the publisher's address, identifying the editor by name if possible.
- Skip a line and type the salutation, using the editor's name (Dear Ms. Smith, or Dear Mary Smith). Use a colon (:) after the name.
- Skip two lines and begin the first paragraph. Tell the editor the titles of the work you are submitting for consideration. In the second paragraph, mention why you are submitting to this particular publication. In the third paragraph, tell the editor something personal about yourself. In the fourth paragraph thank the editor for considering your work.
- Skip two lines before typing a closing salutation — usually the word "Sincerely" followed by a comma.
- Skip four more lines before typing your name, to leave space for your signature.

The cover letter and manuscript go into a #10 or business-size envelope, along with an SASE. Make sure to use the correct postage. Drop the letter in the mail and hope for the best.

Don't expect a quick response. Most publications take over a month to respond to submissions, so don't worry if your poems are not returned quickly. Keep a record of when you mailed your submission and when you expect a reply. (The writers' guidelines should include a response time.) While you wait, keep writing!

PERIODICALS THAT ACCEPT CHILDREN/TEEN/YOUNG ADULT WORK

THE ACORN, 1530 7th St., Rock Island, IL 61201. Phone 309-788-3980. For children and teens. SASE for guidelines.

AMERICAN GIRL MAGAZINE, 8400 Fairway Place, Middleton, WI 53562. Phone 608-836-4848. For 8-12 year old writers. SASE for guidelines.

THE APPRENTICE WRITER, c/o Gary Fincke, Susquehanna University, Selinsgrove, PA 17870-1001. For grades 9-12, primarily from eastern and northeastern states. SASE for guidelines.

BOODLE, P.O. Box 1049, Portland, IN 47371. Phone 219-726-8141.

BROKEN STREETS, 57 Morningside Dr. E., Bristol, CT 06010. Religious publication for children.

BRILLIANT STAR, Baha'i National Center, Wilmette, IL 60091. Religious publication for children 5-14.

CALLIOPE, 7 School St., Peterborough, NH 03458. For children 8-14, history themes.

CHICKADEE & OWL, 179 John St., Suite 500, Toronto, Ontario M5T 3G5, Canada. Science, nature, environment themes.

CLUBHOUSE, P.O. Box 15, Berrien Springs, MI 49103. Ages 9-15.

COBBLESTONE, 7 School St., Peterborough, NH 03458. Phone 603-924-7209. For children, American history themes.

CREATIVE KIDS, P.O. Box 8813, Waco TX 76714. Phone 800-998-2208. For children 5-18.

CRICKET MAGAZINE, P.O. Box 300, Peru, IL 61354. Phone 815-224-6656. For children age 7+.

HOW ON EARTH!, P.O. Box 339, Oxford, PA 19363-0339. Phone 717-529-8638. For ages 13-24. Ecological themes. SASE for guidelines.

INK BLOT, 901 Day Road, Saginaw, MI 48609.

KID'S MAGAZINE, P.O. Box 3041, Grand Central Station, New York, NY 10017. For children 5-15.

THE LOUISVILLE REVIEW, Children's Corner, 315 Bingham Humanities, University of Louisville, Louisville, KY 40292. Phone 502-588-6801. For children and teens.

LADYBUG, Carus Corporation, P.O. Box 300, Peru, IL 61354. Phone 815-224-6643. For children 2-7.

THE MCGUFFEY WRITER, 5128 Westgate Dr., Oxford, OH 45056. Grades K-12.

MERLYN'S PEN: THE NATIONAL MAGAZINE OF STUDENT WRITING, Box 1058, East Greenwich, RI 02818. Phone 800-247-2027. For teens, grades 6-12.

POCKETS, 1908 Grand., P.O. Box 189, Nashville, TN 37202. Phone 615-340-7333. Religious publication for children 6-12.

SKIPPING STONES, P.O. Box 3939, Eugene, OR 97403. Phone 503-342-4956. For children and teens.

SKYLARK, 2200 169th St., Hammond, IN 46323. Phone 219-989-2262. For children and teens.

SPRING TIDES, 824 Stillwood Dr., Savannah, GA 31419. Phone 912-925-8800. For children 5-12.

THE SOW'S EAR POETRY REVIEW, 19535 Pleasant View Drive, Abingdon, VA 24211-6827. Phone 703-628-2651. Regional Appalachia publication for children. SASE for guidelines.

STONE SOUP, P.O. Box 83, Santa Cruz, Ca 95063. Phone 408-426-5557. Children through age 13.

STRAIGHT, 8121 Hamilton Ave., Cincinnati, OH 45231. Religious publication for teens.

THE WRITERS' SLATE, P.O. Box 664, Ottawa, KS 66067. Phone 913-242-0407. Grades K-12. SASE for guidelines.

YOUNG VOICES MAGAZINE, P.O. Box 2321, Olympia, WA 98507. Phone 360-357-4683. For children and teens. SASE for guidelines.

APPENDIX

The Middleground Method in Action

The following examples show the middleground method in action with real students. The responses are based on the "Object Poem" exercise, pages 31-34.

Word Gathering

Example 1

A sixth grade student named Zhong-Min Hu brought an agate to class as his object. His handwritten response to the steps filled two full sheets of paper:

STEP 1. One day at a beach past my home, I went agetting with a friend. At first it was tough. My friend knew if something was an agett or a rock. I kept finding rocks, plain, ordinary, dull rocks. Then I finally found one, when everyone else had a million or so. It turned out to be the only agett I found that day and in my whole life.

STEP 2. The object was small, but smooth. It was very smooth, so I like to rub it against my face. I could see a little light through it. It was covered all over with white. I don't know if this is natural or just paint.

STEP 3. My agget looks weird with its marks, white, and weird stuff inside. The white and natural color mixed looks cool, it's like pictures. This is what my object looks like and feels like.

STEP 4. The object reminds me of me because it is humped like me. It's smooth like my face. Other than this there really isn't much about the agget that reminds me of me. It's skinny, but I'm not very skinny.

STEP 5. It's yellow, a little bit. My parents' skin is sort of yellow. If it had glasses it would remind me of my dad, but it doesn't. It really isn't much like my parents.

STEP 6. This agget means to me a lot because this is about the only neat looking thing I found in my life. When I feel like I never find anything, I can look and thing about my agget. It means a lot to me because I felt proud about it. It's something I found.

STEP 7. It is a yellow-white and white agget.

Example 2

Another sixth grader, Rebecca Lindsay, also responded in two pages:

STEP 1. Near the ocean on the white sands of Hawaii. Sweet breeze. Probably near others similar to it. It can be found in other places, like Mexico, Florida, etc.

STEP 2. It has many textures smooth bumpy rough. It is hard with little ripples of porcelain and points it is brown peach cream white orange tan

STEP 3. it is curvy and smooth in the inside. Like a topo map.

STEP 4. My skin is the same peach in the middle the "skin" is soft in some places. My hair has the same highlights it is a big shell I am a tall big kid?

STEP 5. It has a kind voice like my mother. Is pokey like my dad's beard. It has soft skin like my mother's face and rough like my father's face.

STEP 6. It reminds me of the fun time I had in Mexico. I am glad my mom brought it back from Hawaii. It brings memories and I like to listen to the ocean.

STEP 7. I will name my conch shell, "Rachel" My mom sometimes uses it as a "dinner bell."

(The response to Step 7 shows a common misunderstanding among younger students; they nickname their objects rather than naming them.)

Example 3

A final example by Tibi Girczyc-Blum filled only one sheet of paper:

STEP 1. I found my object in Puerta Vallarta, Mexico, on the beach. It was hot.

STEPS 2 and 3. One side has a man's face on it and underneath the man's face there is a dollar sign and $500 written there. It is silver colored and says "Madero" and 1987. On the other side there is a bird with a snake in its mouth, above that it says "estados unidos Mexicanos." The other one is gold colored and has a woman's face on it and next to that it has $1000, 1989, and says guana de asbaje. On the other side it has a bird with a snake in its mouth. rigid.

STEP 3. It is worth something, like me.

STEP 4. I have two just like I have two parents.

STEP 5. I could buy stuff in Mexico and that I was the one who found it first and not somebody else.

STEP 6. Fred and Frederica they are pecos from Mexico . . .

Extracting a Poem

Example 1

Zhong-Min's first rough draft reads as follows:

One day past the outskirts of
McKinleyville
On a sandy beach
Smooth and ghostly rock
Humped and smooth-faced
Yellowish-white skinned

Holding proudness within it
A small and beautiful agget

Rebecca's reads as follows:

Near the sweet breeze of the ocean
Creamy-white ripples of porcelin
and topo map textures, fine elevations
same gentle voice of my mother
often used to bring memories
beautiful shell

Tibi's first draft:

On the beach in Puerta Vallarta,
Mexico
rigid
it's worth something like me
I have two like I have two parents
that I found it, not somebody else
pecos

Polishing and Revising

Example 1

Zhong-Min turned in his first polished draft with only two changes; he moved "McKinleyville" up to the first line and correctly spelled "agate."

One day past the outskirts of McKinleyville
On a sandy beach
Smooth and ghostly rock
Humped and smooth-faced
Yellowish-white skinned
Holding proudness within it
A small and beautiful agate

My suggestions were that Zhong-Min begin his poem "On a sandy beach." It is a better opening line. The repetition of "smooth" and "smooth-faced" is awkward within such a short poem; I suggested the word "polished" as a replacement for the first usage. I deleted the word "rock." The "ish" in "yellowish" clutters the poem and was replaced by "yellow-white skin." "Proudness" is "pride." I deleted the word "it." The last line works as a naming element. I commented: "Very good work. I suggest a few changes and deletions to make for a smoother reading, to avoid repetition, but mostly I am very happy with this. Good stuff. Very nice."

Zhong-Min's final draft is a very fine accomplishment for a twelve-year old boy:

on a sandy beach
polished and ghostly
humped and smooth-faced
yellow white skin
holding pride within
a small and beautiful agate

Example 2

Rebecca changed her draft so it reads as:

Near the sweet breeze of ocean
peachy ripples of porcelain
and creamy white topo map textures
enjoys the cool depths of the ocean
same gentle voice of my mother
often used to bring back memories
beautiful shell

I suggested the deletion of the preposition "near the," "and" in the third line and "enjoys" in the fourth line. I suggested that "same" be replaced with "the," and that the sixth line be simplified to "brings back memories." I also said that I really liked the "topo map texture" image. I summarized with "Very nice. I made a few changes, suggestions for a smoother reading. See what you think and work on it some more yourself. Good work. Thanks."

Rebecca accepted and rejected some of my advice. The final version of her poem reads:

sweet breeze of ocean
peachy ripples of porcelain
creamy white topo map textures
the cool depths of the water
gentle voice of my mother
brings memories
beautiful shell

Example 3

Tibi's next draft also contained changes:

Walking along the hot sandy beach
The waves crashing against the rocks
I can feel the sun on my back
Silver and gold sparkles and I read excitedly
The warm pesos touching my soft
skin

I suggested "walking along" be replaced with "on." I deleted the two "the's" in the second line as well as the "ing" in "crashing." Articles can often be avoided in poems; they are usually unnecessary and clutter the poem. Gerunds ("ing"-words) force the poem into a passive voice, and better-sounding active alternatives are available. I suggested the third line be cut back to "the sun on my skin" and the fourth line be simplified to "silver and gold sparkles." For the fifth line I suggested: "warm pesos excite the palm of my hand." I suggested that she return to a previous draft for the last line: "I feel like an explosion of firecrackers" — a beautiful simile that makes for a strong last line.

My comments to Tibi were: "I cut out what I thought was unnecessary and brought back your firecracker image, it's really good. See what you think and then play some more. Nice work."

Tibi's final version is an example from a student who was able to break loose from the strict format of the assignment to write a very fine poem:

on the hot sandy beach
waves crash against rocks
the sun on my skin
silver and gold sparkles
warm pesos excite the palm of my hand
I feel like an explosion of firecrackers

About the Authors

Benjamin Green is a second-generation native Californian. He earned his B.A. in Individual Freedom in Contemporary Society from Humboldt State University. He is a widely published poet and prose writer and has conducted poetry writing workshops in California schools for several years.

Anita Punla was born in the Philippines and raised in the San Francisco Bay Area. She has a B.A. in Liberal Studies from San Francisco State University. She is a published poet and an experienced leader of workshops in schools.

Benjamin Green and Anita Punla reside in Trinidad, California, with their daughter She'ifa and their dog Buzz.

OTHER TITLES FROM COTTONWOOD PRESS

A Month of Fundays —
A whole year of games and activities for just about every holiday you've ever heard of, and many that you haven't **$23.95**

Abravocabra
The amazingly sensible approach to teaching vocabulary **$21.95**

Homework's Not Another Word for Something Else to Lose —
Helping students WANT to succeed in school and then setting them up for success **$19.95**

Hot Fudge Monday —
Tasty ways to teach parts of speech to students who have a hard time swallowing anything to do with grammar **$19.95**

Short and Sweet —
Quick creative writing activities that encourage imagination, humor and enthusiasm for writing **$10.95**

Journal Jumpstarts —
Quick topics and tips for journal writing **$7.95**

Ideas that Really Work!
Activities for English and language arts **$21.95**

Surviving Last Period on Fridays and Other Desperate Situations —
Cottonwood game book **$14.95**

Games for English and Language Arts **$18.95**

Did You Really Fall into a Vat of Anchovies? —
Games and activities for English and language arts **$18.95**

ImaginACTION —
Using drama in the classroom, no matter what you teach **$14.95**

Writing Your Life —
Autobiographical writing activities for young people **$14.95**

When They Think They Have Nothing to Write About . . .
Cottonwood composition book **$14.95**

Downwrite Funny
Using students' love of the ridiculous to teach serious writing skills **$18.95**

If They're Laughing. . .
Ideas for using humor effectively in the classroom, even if you're not funny yourself **$12.95**

and more!

Call for a free catalog of practical materials for English and language arts, grades 5-12.

1-800-864-4297

www.cottonwoodpress.com

TO ORDER MORE COPIES OF
BEYOND ROSES ARE RED, VIOLETS ARE BLUE

Please send me ______ copies of *BEYOND Roses Are Red, Violets Are Blue.* I am enclosing $19.95, plus shipping and handling ($4.00 for one book, $2.00 for each additional book). Colorado residents add 60¢ sales tax per book. Total amount $_______.

Name ____

(School — use only if shipping to a school) ______________________________

Address ____

City ______________________ State ______ Zip Code __________

Method of Payment:

❑Payment enclosed ❑Visa/MC/Discover ❑Purchase Order

Credit Card# ________________________Expiration Date __________

Signature ____

Send to:

Cottonwood Press, Inc.
107 Cameron Drive
Fort Collins, CO 80525

1-800-864-4297

www.cottonwoodpress.com

Call for a free catalog of practical materials for English and language arts teachers, grades 5-12.

COTTONWOOD PRESS INC.